MGB

THE COMPLETE STORY

Other Titles in the Crowood AutoClassics Series

MGB

THE COMPLETE STORY

Brian Laban

THE CROWOOD PRESS

First published in 1990 by
The Crowood Press Ltd
Ramsbury, Marlborough
Wiltshire SN8 2HR

www.crowood.com

Paperback edition 2005

This impression 2012

British Library Cataloguing-in-Publication Data
A catalogue record for this book is available from the British
Library.

ISBN 978 1 86126 752 8

The photographs in this book were kindly supplied by The
Motoring Picture Library, Beaulieu

The line drawings on pages 43, 50, 75, 135, 143, 163 and 195
were drawn by Terry Hunns; those on pages 138 and 191 are
reproduced courtesy of British Leyland; and those on pages 17,
18, 22, 199, 202 and 203 are reproduced courtesy of The New
England MG T Register Ltd. The drawing on page 78 is
reproduced courtesy of GKN plc, and the drawing on page 163
is reproduced courtesy of *Autocar & Motor* magazine and
Haymarket Publishing.

Typeset by Avonset, Midsomer Norton

Printed and bound in Malaysia by Times Offset (M) Sdn Bhd

Contents

A BRIEF HISTORY OF THE MGB

1957	Planning for MGA successor starts, with EX205/1 and EX205/2 exercises
1957	Frua EX214 styling exercise completed
1958	Hayter styling prototypes completed in EX205 and EX214/- series, and styling approved
1958–1960	Engineering development continued
May 1960	Designs for MGB finalised
1960–1961	First three prototypes built
May 1962	Pre-production cars built
June 1962	First production Bs built
July 1962	MGA phased out
September 1962	B launched, Roadster only, at Earls Court Show
January 1963	Laycock overdrive option offered
October 1964	Five-bearing engine introduced
October 1965	MGB GT launched, with Salisbury rear axle and front anti-roll bar as standard
November 1966	Front anti-roll bar standardised on Roadster
April 1967	Salisbury rear axle standardised on Roadster
July 1967	MGC production starts
October 1967	MGC launched, in Roadster and GT versions
October 1967	MkII (or Fourth Series) Bs introduced, with all-synchro gearbox and automatic option, in common with C; bodyshell modified to suit; emission control equipment, energy absorbing steering column and revised, padded dash fitted to US market cars
October 1968	MGC rear axle ratio and gearbox ratios revised

September 1969	MGC discontinued
October 1969	Recessed grille models introduced, as Fifth Series; Rostyle wheels standard, wires optional; reclining seats standard
September 1970	Minor improvements including better heating and ventilation system, improved hood; more emission equipment for US models
October 1971	MkIII Bs introduced, with revised dashboard and interior trim, including centre armrest, nylon seat facings; after 1971, bodies were pressed and assembled at Pressed Steel, painted and trimmed at Cowley and assembled at Abingdon
October 1972	All B variants revert to more traditional grille, but with black mesh centre; minor interior and external trim changes; tonneau standardised on Roadster, heated rear screen standardised on GTs
December 1972	First MGB GT V8s built
August 1973	MGB GT V8 launched, in right-hand drive GT form only, for UK market
September 1973	Automatic gearbox option discontinued; underbonnet panel shapes of four-cylinder cars standardised with V8; intermediate energy absorbing bumper overriders fitted to US market cars; radial tyres standardised
September 1974	'Rubber bumper' models introduced to comply with US regs. Cars also had increased ride height for all markets and further emission control equipment for USA, including catalysts for California; overdrive modified; single 12-volt battery replaced twin six-volt system
December 1974	GT withdrawn from US market
May 1975	Limited edition Anniversary model introduced, with special paint and trim package; 750 cars built
June 1975	Overdrive fitted as standard
August 1976	Rear anti-roll bar standardised, front anti-roll bar stiffened; gearlever mounted overdrive switch; lower geared steering with smaller wheel; revised cooling system; interior trim changes including new seat material and dash layout
September 1976	MGB GT V8 discontinued
April 1977	Inertia reel seat belts standardised

September 1979	Announcement on 10 September, 'Black Monday', that B production would cease shortly, and that Abingdon would be closed down and MG name discontinued – leading to large scale organised protests and saving, at least, of MG name. Negotiations for take-over of marque name and B production began and continued for some time with Aston Martin, but project finally abandoned in July 1980 due to lack of financial backing
October 1980	Limited edition series of 1,000 cars (Roadsters and GTs) built to commemorate end of B – mostly sold some time after final production. Very last cars, one Roadster, one GT, completed 23 October 1980. Close-down of Abingdon began immediately, with majority of staff out by December 1980. Equipment and fittings auctioned in March 1981 and factory sold April 1981

Introduction

From its launch in May 1962, the MGB was many things to many people. To some it was simply an affordable sports car, to others, as the concept was extended in October 1965, it became an attainable and practical GT car with occasional room for two small ones in the back. It was a roadster, a racer and a rally car; a family sportster and a huge export winner. To the MG Car Company it was both their biggest ever sales success and, ultimately, their swansong.

As a successor to the ultra-successful MGA, the unit-construction B was a lot more than a single car; it was a move up-market for MG and it came to encompass a whole family of models – from the original roadster, through

First of the breed, the classic B Roadster, as launched in September 1962 – in this case with the optional wire wheels which the designers hated.

the elegant, Pininfarina-styled B GT, to the disastrously unpopular six-cylinder C and the excellent but sadly under-exploited V8.

In the eighteen and a half years up to October 1980, when the last B rolled off the Abingdon production lines, MG sold more than half a million examples of the B in its various guises, making it comfortably the best selling sports car of its generation, and they might have gone on selling modern up-dates of the B long beyond that had they been allowed to give the car the development it so badly lacked in its later years.

The problem was not that the market no longer *wanted* a sportscar from MG, neither was it a lack of design skill or engineering talent *within* MG; the men who had made the B work in the first place could have assured its survival through bringing it up to date; and the management at MG could un-doubtedly have saved the B, in spirit if not actually in name, had they been allowed to by the giant British Leyland (BL) con-glomerate of which they had become a part in 1968.

There were more far-reaching plans at Abingdon at the time, too; for an adaptable car that with different engines could have replaced both the B and the smaller Midget; and for a spectacular mid-engined sports car with four- or six-cylinder options that might well have become the MGD.

But it was not to be. BL's antipathy towards MG, latterly in favour of corporate sports car rivals Triumph, let the B stagnate. That stagnation led to a slipping reputation and plummetting sales, especially in the vital and hitherto lucrative US market where MG latterly had the twin nightmares of snowballing safety requirements and a horribly unfavourable sterling/dollar ex-change rate.

By the early 1970s the B was effectively doomed. The proposed 1970 replacement was abandoned and the ageing old stager was asked to soldier on with little support and little real development other than the negative forms that were forced upon it by that stricter US legislation.

By 1979 British Leyland were in deep trouble overall, and MG – not for the first time in their turbulent history – became a foil for big company politics. So the B went, and Abingdon went with it, a redundant plant which had no place in Leyland's future plans in spite of its huge contribution to motoring history.

Sentiment had no place in Leyland either – not in the upper echelons at least; in finally abandoning the B and any plans for an MG successor, Leyland effectively killed a sports car tradition stretching back to the 1920s.

The next time the MG badge appeared it was on a mildly uprated Metro saloon, and although MG enthusiasts around the world universally craved another real MG sports car, it would be over a decade before the MG*F* appeared. Launched in 1995, the mid-engined two-seater effectively revived the marque, which is the jewel in Rover's crown today, but the B and all its fascinatingly var-ied family is still hugely appreciated for what it is – an honest, down-to-earth sports car for the masses, in the finest MG tradition.

This is its story, and we have approached it in as logical a way as possible, starting with a look at the roots of the MG tradition and the man who created the marque, Cecil Kimber.

We look at the B's heritage, and at the way its antecedents set the scene for MG's best-ever seller – with particular attention of course to cars like the T-Series, which opened up the American market, and the A, which finally took MG into the modern, stream-lined era.

We look at the people who created the cars, many of them, like Syd Enever and John Thornley, involved from the earliest days right through to the end; we look in great detail at how the B evolved from the first sketches through styling models, rejects and rethinks to become a production project with a pressing launch date; and we look at the

Whitewall tyres and left-hand drive identify a car for the US market in this first series of press release pictures.

place where most of their work was done: Abingdon.

The competition history of the B and its derivatives is dealt with in its own chapter, as are owning, driving, restoring and maintaining the various cars. We look at the clubs which cater for B owners and enthusiasts around the world, and at the options now open for keeping the car in pristine condition – or even building a 'new' B from scratch.

Inevitably, we have to analyse what went wrong in the end, and whether it could have been avoided; and we look at what might have been, in the shape of possible B replacements that never progressed beyond the prototype stage.

Most of all, of course, we look at the cars themselves, from before their launch to after their demise. This includes concept, development, introduction and popular reception, the running changes, and the eventual phasing out. By treating each of the major series (B Roadster, B GT, C Roadster and C GT, and GT V8) in separate chapters, we have included the maximum possible amount of information in the clearest possible way.

*The first attempt at a bigger engined derivative, the C, was a
failure in sales terms after a very bad initial reception from the
specialist press.*

Left: *The 1975 BGT V8 with rubber
bumpers combines the best and the
worst of the B story: the GT shape
was a hugely successful extension to
the family and the V8 engine gave all
the power the B could ever need, but
there was never a V8 Roadster and
the rubber bumpers marked the
beginning of the end.*

And where it's appropriate, we hope we
haven't been afraid to say that some things
about the B were clearly wrong; this is an
affectionate look, but not a eulogy.

Going into the second decade after the B
finally bowed out, it has never been more
sought after. Understand the real story of
the B and it isn't difficult to see why . . .

1 The MG Philosophy and the B Heritage

'There is no sure blueprint for the creation of a great classic motorcar. Yet all true classics have qualities in common that are evident at a glance: a clean, graceful and timeless look; rare poise in motion and a sure feeling that it was conceived by motoring enthusiasts and built by dedicated craftsmen.

'In view of the fact that few authentic classics have ever been created since the evolution of the motorcar, it is little short of astonishing to contemplate how many of them are MGs.

'Today's MGB may well be the finest expression of the MG philosophy. It is clean, lean and quick to respond. It is satisfying to look at and great fun to drive. Equipped as it is with rack and pinion steering, short-throw four-speed stick with optional overdrive, track-bred suspension, radial tires, lively 1798cc engine and power-assisted disc/drum brakes, the MGB has reflexes that match your own. It all adds up to a very contemporary classic, the best selling convertible sportscar in America. Find out how it feels to be part of a great classic sportscar tradition. Drive the wide-open MGB today . . . '

That advertising copy appeared in the US media in the autumn of 1979, under the heading 'MGB: THE CLASSIC BREED'. It carried the emotive MG octagon, of course, and showed the latest edition of the B Roadster (in left-hand drive form) photo-graphed in rolling English countryside, in front of a group of earlier T-series cars, a small band of Owners Club enthusiasts and a young lady in a terribly English tweed hat. Jaguar Rover Triumph Inc, of Leonia NJ, were obviously still pushing tradition for all it was worth.

One of the places where that advertisement appeared was on the back cover of the Fall 1979 edition of the *MG Magazine* – Volume 1 Number 3 of the 'Official Publication for MG Owners', published for the aforementioned Jaguar Rover Triumph Inc in co-operation with the MG Car Clubs in North America. In the same issue, the news pages announced the 1980 B models, including an Exclusive New 'Limited Edition' MGB convertible, as unveiled shortly before at the New York Show; elsewhere in the issue, there is a reprinted editorial column from the *New York Times* of 12 September 1979, on the love of sports car motoring – and on some worrying news from England about America's favourite, the MG.

And the *MG Magazine*'s own editorial page in that same issue was headed 'A Fond Farewell to Abingdon', opening with the ominous paragraph: 'Since our last issue in the summer, there have been some fundamental business changes which will affect the future of MG cars . . . '

The MGB, the biggest selling sports car of all time in its heyday, and a car which had been treated with everything from reverence to ridicule in its time, was finally coming to the end of its eighteen-year, 500,000-car production run, and people were suddenly starting to realise just how much they would miss it.

The story of the MGB is a story of achievement against all the odds, of sales and competition success and of critical acclaim, of individual genius, and of corporate indifference on such a frightening scale that the product (and even the marque) was ultimately doomed.

And in the story of the B, there is a distillation of the story of MG itself – the same success against the odds, the same acclaim, the same genius and the same vulnerability to corporate fickleness, running right through the marque's history. Even the B's survival into the 1980s, when it might easily have died five or even ten years earlier, is typical of that MG durability.

Certainly, MG's history is dotted with some exceptional individual models, and many remarkable racing and record breaking achievements, but, overall, MG's image is as a builder of sports cars for the people.

In much the same way that MG was never the most glamorous marque, the B may never have been the world's greatest sports car, but to even the most inexpert eye it was everything that sports car motoring should be about: a straightforward car with purposeful lines and sparkling performance, a car full of character that was accessible and above all was *fun*.

If you're looking for a definition of 'sports car', the B is surely close to it.

In effect, it was only MG's second 'modern' sportscar line – taking the all-enveloping body style which MG had finally adopted with the highly successful A, and adding both creature comforts and the modern manufacturing methods of unit construction. From the moment the B was first shown to the public, in Roadster-only guise at the London Motor Show at Earls Court in 1962, it was another MG success story.

When it was launched, after around four years of development led by Sydney Enever and John Thornley, MG themselves expected the B to last for no longer than perhaps seven years. And it seems very unlikely that they could ever have *dreamed* that the B and its derivatives would eventually sell more than half a million cars around the world – a figure comfortably bigger than the total production of all other MG models since the firm's piecemeal beginnings.

FIRM FOUNDATIONS

In the MG A, certainly, the new B had a firm foundation to build on. That model had also taken MG to new heights of sales success, with a total of over 100,000 cars sold – and well over eighty per cent of those had gone to the USA.

That US market strength, which started in a modest way with the TC, was the real secret of MG's massive post-war expansion and considerable commercial success – and it was the reason why the B too would sell in such enormous numbers.

Yet when the last MGB rolled off the Abingdon production lines, on 23 October 1980, it was largely the dependence on that dominant US export market that had finally sealed MG's fate. The combination of slipping sales, tougher safety and emissions rules and a dreadful sterling/dollar relationship (from a UK exporter's point of view, at least) marked more than just the end of another model, it effectively marked the end of the MG tradition – at least for the foreseeable future.

Where the tinge of sadness at the end of a long and successful run is normally tempered by the challenge of building something new and better, the workers at Abingdon had no bright future to look forward to, only a glorious past to mourn.

And that past was something else that the September 1979 *New York Times* editorial had recognised, when it said:

'The MG was more than another handsome car; it was a symbol of freedom for the first generation of young, middle-class Americans able to buy personal cars. Not overstuffed family sedans with portholes and fold-down armrests but open two-seat roadsters, hard-riding, quick-cornering – the kind of car one's mother couldn't get into even if she wanted to, which she most certainly did not. Sports cars they were called . . .'

The man who started the MG philosophy, Cecil Kimber, would have been proud to know that he got it right. Even though his own association with the marque had ended long before the B was ever dreamed of (and so, tragically, had his life), the B, and especially the V8, would probably have pleased him too. He simply loved sports cars and it is impossible to talk about even the post-war cars without acknowledging Kimber and the spirit that he built.

CECIL KIMBER AND THE EARLY DAYS

Although most people automatically associate Kimber with Abingdon (and the name is a common one around Oxford), he was born on 12 April 1888 in Dulwich, in south-east London, where his father, Henry Francis Kimber, was a partner in the family printing engineering business – and also, it seems, a fairly stern Victorian patriarch.

From Dulwich, Kimber senior moved, via nearby Merton and Streatham, to open a new printing inks business in Stockport, Lancashire, in 1896.

He took the whole family with him. Cecil completed his education at Stockport Grammar School, and both he and his brother Vernon (six years his junior) eventually went to work for their father, but Cecil did so only under some duress. He worked as a salesman, but his real interests were already

Cecil Kimber, the man behind the marque.

elsewhere – largely in things mechanical, and especially in motor cycles.

The man who created MG never had any formal engineering training, though – and what he did learn he learned from working on his own motor cycles, starting with a 1906, belt-driven Rex and progressing as quickly as he could afford, always to faster models.

In 1910, his two-wheeler enthusiasm was almost the end of him, when he was involved in a low-speed accident at a crossroads, with a car driven by a local stockbroker. Kimber

Kimber Arms
Frangas Non Flectes

The Kimber coat of arms: the motto means 'Break but not bend'.

smashed his right leg so badly that it seemed certain that he would lose it. He didn't, but he spent a very long time in and out of hospital having the leg rebuilt, with a plate permanently holding his right thigh together, a couple of inches difference between his good leg and the shattered one, and a heavy limp which he carried for the rest of his life.

His disability was enough to have him rejected for military service when World War I began, and, indirectly, it was also what launched him into his motor industry career.

His mother died while he was being tended in hospital, he chose to spend some of the compensation money he received after the accident on buying his first car (a Singer Ten) instead of putting it into the now struggling family business, and by 1914 his father had disowned him.

In 1915, Kimber married the daughter of an engineer from Manchester and, around the same time, went to work as assistant to the chief engineer at Sheffield–Simplex, a small but respected car maker based in Sheffield.

Soon after that he moved south again, to work for some two years as a buyer with AC Cars in Thames Ditton – the one-time commercial vehicle builder just starting their own career as a manufacturer of sporting cars.

In 1919, Kimber moved on again – this time to become 'works organiser' for gearbox and axle manufacturers E G Wrigley, in Birmingham. Through Wrigleys he became involved in the Angus–Sanderson car project, styling the radiator for a car which Angus Sanderson were assembling in Newcastle-upon-Tyne around 1918 and 1919 – and also apparently losing the balance of his compensation money through backing the promising but ultimately abortive Angus–Sanderson project.

That was the negative side, the positive side was that through Wrigleys he also met one William Richard Morris of Oxford, who was already becoming a motor manufacturer of some standing.

THE MORRIS CONNECTION

While Kimber was still not much more than a peripatetic industry jack-of-all-trades, Morris was the archetypal self-made man. He started with a bicycle repair business in his garden shed (allegedly after being refused a pay rise of a shilling a week by his original employer), graduated through motor cycle repairs to two- and four-wheel salesman, first as The Oxford Garage and then, in 1910 and growing rapidly, as the Morris Garage.

A couple of years later, still expanding, that became Morris Garages, and the proprietor looked to his next obvious avenue for expansion – manufacture. He eventually became the biggest motor manufacturer in Britain – first knighted as Sir William Morris and later ennobled as Lord Nuffield. Having started his business with savings of around £4, he not only built that vast empire, but ultimately went on to donate some £27 million to various charities – and through it all he never lost the apparently penny-pinching habit of rolling his own cigarettes!

Morris started as a manufacturer by building a prototype car, with proprietary engine and largely bought-in running gear, at his Longwall Street sales garage in 1913.

That quickly went into production in nearby Cowley, as the 'Bullnose' Morris Oxford, and by the time Morris met Kimber, the Oxford was well on its way to becoming Britain's best-selling car – with Wrigleys as one of the major suppliers.

Morris, through keeping close personal track on *all* his suppliers, met a lot of people like Kimber, but in 1921 Kimber was the one he wanted to become sales manager for Morris Garages, which was now, of course, a major sales outlet for Morris's own cars.

The Morris Garages showrooms, where Kimber became general manager in 1922, starting the MG story.

But Morris Garages was having an unsettled time as Kimber arrived; the first manager, F G Barton, had resigned in 1919, due to ill health, and his place had been taken by Edward Armstead, who had previously been involved with Morris's bicycle and motor cycle operation. In March 1922, not long after Kimber had gone to Oxford, Armstead suddenly resigned, and within a couple of months had committed suicide.

Kimber was quickly appointed as general manager and this gave him a great deal of scope to pursue more ambitious plans – and what's more, Morris (who was not widely known for giving his employees a lot of freedom to do things outside of their normal remit) seemed prepared to let him.

And that, in effect, was the springboard for the launch of MG.

Kimber's own philosophy was that there was a market for a car costing markedly more than standard if its performance or handling or appearance were markedly better. He started by rebodying a series of 11.9hp Hotchkiss-engined Cowleys with what he called 'Chummy' coachwork, on slightly modified chassis and with better trim; and late in 1923 he added a more sporting two-seater version of the Cowley, buying in six 'sports' bodies from a local coach-builders, Raworth, and fitting them to almost standard chassis during 1923 and 1924.

The rather slow sales reflected the fact that Kimber's sporty car was around twice the price of a standard Cowley and not really special enough to justify the difference, and the four-seater Chummy also had a rival by the end of 1923, in the form of a similar but much cheaper model from Morris himself – the Occasional Four.

THE BIRTH OF MG

If Kimber was rattled he didn't show it, but instead introduced several permutations of *his* Cowley and Oxford based specials, some with more power, most with some body innovation.

In March 1924 an advertisement appeared in *The Morris Owner* for the 'M.G. Saloon', the first time that the initials had appeared to identify Kimber's cars, which until then had simply been Morris Garages Specials.

The obvious inference, then and forever after, was that M.G. (or MG) stood for Morris

Early days at Cowley, with 18/80s chassis leaving the works in 1929, en route for Carbodies in Coventry.

The archetypal MG sports car: C-type Midgets on the production line in 1931.

Garages. In fact the company made a fairly unequivocal statement to that effect in 1929, saying: 'Out of compliment to Sir William R Morris, Bt, we named our production the MG Sports, the letters being the initials of his original business undertaking, "The Morris Garages", from which has sprung the vast group of separate enterprises including the MG Car Co'.

Kimber's daughter, on the other hand, has said that her father himself always maintained that they stood for neither Morris Garages nor for anything else in particular, but could just stand for themselves; which undoubtedly said more for his attitude to the marque than to its commercial status!

ENTER THE OCTAGON

The next link in MG folklore was the famous octagon badge, which again appeared in an advertisement before it appeared on any car – this time in May 1924's edition of *The Morris Owner*, for the MG Super Sports Morris. And when Kimber introduced his handsome 1925 model tourer on the new, longer Oxford 14/28 chassis, there was no further reference to the Morris origins and it was simply advertised as the MG Super Sports.

But the most famous link of all is certainly the car which will always be known as 'Old Number One'. It had neither the MG name nor the octagon on its bull nose (it had the round badge of the Morris Garages, Oxford) but the famous logo *did* appear on its side, and even Kimber subsequently acknowledged it as the first real MG in the true spirit of the marque.

The car was built for the Easter 1925 Lands End Trial, and was started sometime late in 1924, in the Longwall Street workshop – with no intended purpose other than that competition.

Based on a shortened and heavily modified Cowley chassis, and with a rare overhead-valve Hotchkiss engine, it had a slim and pretty two-seater body with staggered seating to keep the width down, and rudimentary cycle type wings. It was finished in March but broke its chassis as it was being tested – calling for a rapid repair at Alfred Lane the day before the Trial started.

The effort paid off in a gold medal for Kimber and his passenger, Wilfred Matthews, but the car, registered FC 7900, was sold soon after, as Kimber was already thinking of his next project.

'Old Number One' was eventually bought back by the MG company in the 1930s, virtually as scrap, was rebuilt, repainted in red rather than the original dark grey, and has spent the years since as an exhibition piece and an anachronism for historians and enthusiasts to argue over endlessly – on the basis that the MG ethos was clearly becoming established well before 'Old Number One' ever turned a wheel.

Kimber in the battle-stained Lands End Trials car which, for better or worse, became known as 'Old Number One'.

Evolution of the MG badge, from early days with Cowleys and the Morris Garages to the famous octagon.

THE MG TRADITION

Whatever else the arguments show, they do show the depth of feeling about MG tradition, and there's no denying that this was the time when MG's fortunes really began to take off. This is not the place to record the whole complex history in between, but a brief outline does help to put the B and its modern cousins into perspective.

Probably no more than half a dozen men had ever worked on 'MGs' at the 2,000 sq ft former stable workshop in Alfred Lane, but by September 1925 demand was strong enough for Kimber to have to ask Morris (who was still the proprietor, it should be remembered) for more space.

He found it in one bay of the Morris radiator works in Bainton Road, but by September 1927 they had outgrown that factory too, and moved to a brand new building (financed by Morris) in Edmund Road, Cowley – where the first Midgets were produced, in 1928.

The Midget was beautifully timed to adopt the overhead-cam Wolseley engine, as

Morris had bought the fiscally bankrupt but technically rich Wolseley company in 1927. It was the model that launched MG into mass production, the first MG to sell more than 1,000 examples in a year and the start of the 'popular' line which led to the modern Midget and the B itself.

By this time, the company was 'The MG Car Co (Proprietors: The Morris Garages Ltd)', and, in spirit at least, was growing apart from Morris products – and once the overhead-cam era began, Kimber's ambitions were clearly beginning to stretch a long way beyond what the essentially conservative William Morris might originally have had in mind.

Of course, there was a limit; MG, even if it looked to have a deal of independence, was still actually owned by Morris at this point, and as such was uncomfortably vulnerable to outside management decisions.

But at least it was still growing, and in September 1929 the company moved to the factory that is almost synonymous with it, and where all the Bs were eventually built: Abingdon.

ABINGDON AND THE
MG CAR CO

The works at Abingdon, about six miles out of Oxford and on the Thames, was a disused factory adjoining the Pavlova Leather Co's works, which Morris had previously utilised for storing used cars. Pavlova had expanded into the extra space during World War I when they made leather coats in huge numbers for the army, but although they stayed in business after the war they no longer needed quite so much room.

The move was celebrated with a change of name to simply The MG Car Co, and with a big lunch at the works on 20 January 1930. On 17 July a small printed notice was issued which simply said '. . . owing to the phenomenal increase in the volume of business carried on by the MG Car Co . . .', a separate

Ltd Co was being formed; on 21 July 1930 MG finally became The MG Car Co Ltd, with Sir William Morris as governing director and Cecil Kimber as managing director.

For some years, MG's success story encompassed production cars (having once weathered the general depression of 1931), record breaking, and motor racing – especially with the fabulously successful K3 Magnette. But at the same time, MG was under constant pressure to be a financially viable part of the Morris empire, and that culminated in July 1935 with Lord Nuffield (as Morris became in 1934) selling MG (plus Wolseley) out of his private domain and into the publicly owned Morris Motors, relegating Kimber to the position of general manager and director.

That marked the end of MG's racing programme (but never quite stifled the record

Racing was always an on/off occupation for MG, dependent on prevailing parent company politics, but the record breakers were very hard to stifle. This 1938 shot of Major Goldie Gardner's 1,100cc car shows Kimber on the left, with Lord Nuffield, Gardner and Reid Railton.

breaking) and forced a switch from the lovely overhead-cam Wolseley-type engines to Morris's 'parts-bin' pushrod units – all under the instigation of managing director Leonard Lord, and in the interests of rationalisation. It also marked the closing of the Abingdon design office, with MG design being centralised at Cowley, not to return to Abingdon until the early 1950s.

It says a lot for the resilience of the MG name that the company survived, and more than that grew steadily up to World War II, with cars like the first of the famous T-Series turning MG into the biggest sports car manufacturer in the world.

Car production stopped completely when war did come (although that wasn't the case throughout the industry, with some manufacturers maintaining production for military needs). At first, Abingdon inexplicably found it very difficult to find war work of any kind, though they did eventually start to produce all manner of military hardware, from tanks to aircraft parts.

The works escaped enemy bombing, the worst of its wartime problems being a fire in 1944, but sadly one of the war contracts brought about the departure of Cecil Kimber.

MG AFTER KIMBER

Early in the war, in 1941, Kimber negotiated a contract for Abingdon's skilled workforce to build the complex nose sections of the Albemarle bomber, but Miles Thomas, the forceful new vice chairman of what had now become the Nuffield Organisation, objected to Kimber having acted independently from what he dictated should be a centralised war effort.

The clash was symptomatic of the friction between the autonomously-minded Kimber and the inflexible Thomas, and Kimber officially 'resigned', virtually on the spot.

He never built another car, but worked

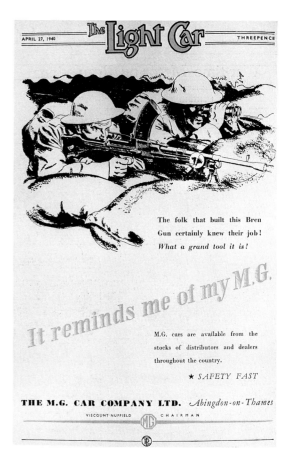

The MG spirit survived the war, but Kimber didn't; sacked from the company in 1941, he was killed in a freak rail accident in February 1945.

first for former coachbuilders Charlesworths, organising war work, and then for Specialloid Pistons as works director.

It was on business for Specialloid that Kimber left Kings Cross station on the evening of 4 February 1945, and was killed in a freak rail accident. His train began to slip backwards on a steep incline, two carriages were derailed and Kimber and one other passenger were killed.

Not long before, he had been talking to John Black, the chairman of the Standard Motor Co, about a possible future with the Triumph sports car division. There is surely a certain irony in the possibility that had Kimber gone back to motor manufacturing after the war he might have been involved in the marque which eventually contributed so much to the downfall of the B and of MG itself . . .

As for MG, the company was very quick to get production under way again once the war had finished, with a mildly updated version of the pre-war TB, which logically enough became the TC.

Introduced in October 1945, it was one of the first cars to be built in post-war Britain – and thanks to Nuffield's Morris Industries Exports branch it had ready-made access to vital export markets. Without them, the TC could not have happened, as post-war govern-ment policy was 'export or die' – and a car maker who wasn't exporting simply didn't get the steel to build more cars.

FOUNDATIONS FOR THE B

Nowadays, most people think of the TC as the car that opened up America to MG in par-ticular, and to British and European sports cars in general. It did, too, but it went to Commonwealth countries like Australia and South Africa even before the first US exports started in 1947.

America, of course, still had a war in the Pacific to worry about, but the TC really took

MG were very quickly back onto the market after World War II, with the lovely little TC.

Company politics delayed the MGA by a couple of years, but once it arrived the first 'modern' MG was a major success. This is a 1959 MGA 1600.

off when GIs started coming back from Europe with their sporty little cars as personal imports. It didn't take a genius to see that the tiny, relatively underpowered MGs could run rings around the lumbering domestic saloons of the time, which spelt fun – and the sort of freedom that the war veterans had been fighting for. MGs also became prominent in road racing as that sport took off in the USA too – another sign of tastes changed by exposure to European ways.

Yet the numbers involved were not exactly enormous in the early days. In total, the TC sold exactly 10,000 copies between the end of 1945 and late 1949, and only around 1,800 of those went to the USA. That's large as a percentage to a single market when MG's total export market pre-war had only been between fifteen and twenty per cent, but it was still really only a drop across the ocean.

What's more, the Nuffield management seemed strangely nervous about the success.

On the one hand, chief executive Sir Miles Thomas told *The Autocar* magazine in March 1947 that of all their vehicles, he intended to market only MGs in the USA, because 'it has a playboy appeal quite different from anything they make'; on the other hand, Nuffield undertook virtually no advertising for MGs in the USA and was apparently so reluctant to risk the investment needed to open up the potentially vast market that

The TC paved the way for the TD which opened up the US market for MG in a huge way in the early 1950s.

Nuffield dithered again with the B, and its launch in 1962 was only just in time. Most early cars, like this one, were US bound.

sales outlets were franchised to the trading side of bankers Hambros, and they financed the expansion.

OPENING UP THE MARKET

Whatever the reticence, the market grew rapidly. When MG introduced the still traditionally styled but very much updated TD, in 1954, it had not only a new chassis, better brakes, independent front-suspension and more room, it also had the option of left-hand drive. And America went wild for it, with around eighty per cent of the TD's near 30,000 production (a record for MG up to that time) actually crossing the Atlantic.

While that was obviously exceptionally good in most respects, it gave MG a problem in that the US market did have a pretty big say in what sort of cars the company built

This 1970 Roadster is not alone in reverting to the earlier 'traditional' grille, and the message was not lost on MG, but real changes were too often left too late.

next; and once the novelty of the back-to-basics fun had worn off a bit, that meant a steady demand for more comfort and sophistication.

In truth, the next model, the TF, introduced in 1953, wasn't nearly good enough.

Once again, MG had found themselves at the mercy of a corporate reshuffle. In 1952, the Nuffield Organisation (including MG, of course) merged with the Austin Motor Company to form the British Motor Corporation (BMC). And this time, MG were faced with a corporate boss who was not so much indifferent as downright hostile.

He was Leonard Lord, the same Leonard Lord who had taken away Kimber's overhead-cam engines back in 1935 when Nuffield sold MG into the Morris Motors fold. In the interim, Lord had been sacked by Nuffield from his position as vice chairman of Morris Motors, had joined Austin and become chairman, and was now in control of the whole new BMC organisation.

It would be simplistic to say that Lord operated any kind of vendetta against MG, or against any other of the Morris elements of the new corporation, but he certainly wasn't going to be unduly helpful. One of his first moves after the merger was to reject a possible TD replacement, in favour of what became the Austin–Healey 100 – with 2.6-litre Austin A90 engine.

The MG prototype was EX175, a new type of MG with a streamlined body instead of the 'traditional' T-series type, and just the sort of car that America was crying out for. Lord could see room for only one corporate sports car within the BMC game plan of the time, though, and his newly created Austin–Healey was going to be it. MG were restricted to building another mildly uprated T-Series, the sadly outdated and slow-to-sell TF, and EX175 was put under wraps for some three years. EX175, had it happened at the time, would have been the MGA prototype . . .

2 The MGA – First Link to the B

Considering the company's long standing involvement with streamlined record breakers, it is perhaps surprising that it took MG so long to produce a 'modern' streamlined sports car for the road. Tradition, in the shape of cars like the T-Series, had really had its day by the beginning of the 1950s, especially in the USA. A society which now expected the streamlined shape of modern aeroplanes to be reflected even in family saloons, was rapidly growing out of sit-up-and-beg sports cars with flowing wings and slab fuel tanks, even if they were MGs.

By 1952, the customers were voting with their feet and showing MG that they really didn't want a car like the TD any more; but, for a while at least, MG didn't seem to listen. Or, to be more accurate, MG's new masters at BMC didn't.

As ever, it wasn't that the MG people were short of ideas, rather that they were short of corporate support and the one spark of life that turns ideas into products.

There was one suggestion that BMC might have been coming round before the launch of the stop-gap TF, but even this showed that they were still hedging their bets.

It was a prototype that appeared in 1953, and it was a car that could have used either updated 'traditional' styling, with flowing wings *à la* T-Series, or it could appear with much more modern, streamlined bodywork. The change was made possible by the simple expedient of using a basic inner shell with bolt-on outer panels. The 'traditional' shell frankly looked like the compromise that it was, but the 'modern' one (even with the shared upright grille) was really quite attractive, in a chunky way not unlike very early Ferrari *barchettas*. And not totally unlike the later B . . .

It was a Cowley project, of course, emanating from Gerald Palmer's office there that oversaw all official MG design at the time, but it never went beyond the mock-up stage.

THE BACK-DOOR ROUTE

Fortunately for BMC, perhaps, MG's own designers weren't quite as dormant at this time as they were strictly meant to be – especially when it came to record breaking and racing. The record breaking had gone on as a 'back-door' activity more or less at any time that it was frowned on officially; and with the skills of Syd Enever very much in the forefront, it had been enormously successful and prestigious. The racing, on the other hand, really had been outlawed since the war. H A Ryder, the man responsible for MG at Cowley in those days, held staunchly to the Nuffield line that racing was a waste of time and money and had no place in this particular organisation.

S V Smith, who succeeded Ryder at Cowley from December 1947, was officially bound to the same line, but he wasn't quite so diligent at watching what went on 'unofficially'. What he didn't know about he could hardly be expected to stamp on.

He obviously chose not to know too much at

George Phillips finished second in his class with his privately rebodied TC at Le Mans in 1950, and went to MG for something better for 1951.

first about the streamlined TD-based car that Syd Enever and Alec Hounslow were working on early in 1951 for *Autosport* photographer George Phillips to run at Le Mans in mid-June.

Phillips, a one-time Fleet Street despatch rider, was becoming a Le Mans regular with MGs. He'd raced a special bodied TC there in 1949 – a car with rounded bodywork, cycle wings and a big curved windscreen. And he'd finished second in class with his rebodied TC in 1950. He went to Abingdon looking for 'something pretty and effective' for 1951 – based on a lightened TD because there wasn't much else, but at least streamlined enough to be effective on the long Mulsanne Straight.

What he got was the instantly recognisable forerunner of the MGA, a project which Alec Hounslow and the inevitable Enever launched into early in 1951 with a mixture of stealth and gusto.

Enever styled it with obvious reference to his record breakers – notably EX135 – but with the practicalities of road racing superimposed. His drawings were translated into quarter-scale models by Harry Herring in the Abingdon body shop and tested in the Armstrong Whitworth wind tunnel in Coventry – fortuitously without having to ask Coventry to pay the bills because Enever had wartime connections with Armstrong.

A MEASURE OF APPROVAL

At first, the work was actually kept hidden completely from Smith, to the extent that the half-built car was wheeled out of the works whenever he visited. When the light alloy body was built, though, and Smith *was* told about the car, he gave his blessing – to go with that of MG's then managing director, Jack Tatlow.

Enever and Hounslow had done a magnificent job for Phillips. Just like the A which followed, the car had beautiful and obviously aerodynamically effective lines – spoilt only by the hump in the bonnet for the tall XPAG engine of the TD, and the way the narrow chassis from the same source dictated a high driving position which had the driver sticking well up into the airstream.

Even so, the car was pretty quick; it recorded 116mph (187kph) on the Mulsanne and lapped steadily at around 80mph (129kph) for some sixty laps before being forced out with a piston failure and attendant bent valves.

Phillips blamed MG for that, and apparently when they offered him the car he refused it.

Enever wasn't so anti EX172, as the project had been known. He could see the streamlined production car in it that MG so badly needed; but he had to do something about that unfortunate driving position. What forced that upon him was the TD's narrow chassis, which obliged the driver and

*Tall TD engine remains, but Enever's wide chassis gives room
to drop seats on the next stage towards the A.*

*Final A prototype made its debut at Le Mans in June 1955,
with 1,489cc 82bhp engine and almost standard A look.*

MGA on test, with a Pininfarina A40 dead ahead:
Pininfarina's involvement with BMC continued with the B GT.

passenger to sit above, rather than inside, the line of the chassis side members.

The eminently practical Enever therefore took the only route possible and drew up a new chassis with rails swept far enough apart from behind the scuttle area for him to drop the seats low down between them.

That meant that he wouldn't have to give the car such a high windscreen for road use and by raising the sides slightly he could give it a totally civilised cockpit. In fact by 1950s' sports car standards it was almost palatial, simply trimmed but with an enormous amount of leg room and extraordinarily generous scope for seat adjustment for even the tallest driver.

He quickly had two examples of the new chassis fabricated, based on deep box section rails with strong crossmembers and a massive hoop for the front bulkhead to mount on. It was heavy, but it was stiff enough to leave the body unstressed, which in turn meant that it could be relatively simple to make; and simple meant cheap.

Herring made the styling model for the wind tunnel, keeping the pretty grille which EX172 had had, and BMC's body branch in Coventry turned it into a full size car – in incredibly quick time.

Within three months, by late 1952, EX175 was complete, and road registered as HMO 6. It was fully trimmed and under the skin everything except the all-important chassis was derived from the TD, including the tall 1,250 XPAG engine, which meant the road-going prototype had to have a bonnet bulge just like the racer.

Tatlow loved it and MG presented it to the now BMC management as their putative replacement for the ageing TD.

They were just days too late to turn the EX175 into the A there and then. Leonard Lord had fallen for the new Healey 100 sports car at the London Motor Show some three days earlier and had already committed Austin to building that as their new corporate sports car. He didn't need another.

MG had developed EX175 apparently oblivious of the fact that Lord had virtually put the new car out to tender – letting it be known among various small manufacturers that a sports car that could be built cheaply around surplus Austin A90 running gear would be keenly received by the company.

That was excellent news for Healey, but a disaster for MG, who had to go back and revamp the TD as best they could on a shoestring budget.

Part of Lord's reasoning had presumably been that the TD was still selling quite strongly at this time, but he'd rather shot himself in the foot with the Healey in one

The A was low, modern and stylish, but with exceptional interior space. There wasn't much boot, though, and virtually no security.

respect, as it not unnaturally knocked a big hole in TD sales, especially exports. In fact, after the Healey launch, TD sales fell by close to a half and a mere revamp wasn't about to reverse that.

THORNLEY BITES THE BULLET

One of the few things in MG's favour at the time was that all this coincided with John Thornley's elevation to general manager of the MG Division of BMC. It must have been hard for Thornley to watch the TF being justifiably out-sold by the much more modern Healey (which Abingdon even went on to build from 1957) and it couldn't have been much fun to see the TF's launch at the 1953 Motor Show even further upstaged by the arrival of the new Triumph TR2.

The final uprating of the TF as the TF1500 was hardly likely to achieve very much, but at least it seems that Lord had recognised the problem by now. For Thornley, Enever and his team, that meant EX175 came out of retirement in June 1954 and had to be turned into a production car with a planned launch in April 1955!

At least Lord allowed the Abingdon design office to reopen on the strength of it, which was a significant political victory . . . but the A *did* have to grow up around corporate parts such as the new B-Series engine and transmission.

Enever had used up the second EX175-type chassis long ago for the EX179 record breaker, so there wasn't much to work on to

Abingdon lines had changed little by the A's time and the car still had separate chassis and body.

Detachable works hardtop for the A, introduced in 1956, showed that MG were always aware of another potential market.

start with. Fortunately, EX175 was so close to how everyone wanted to see the final car appear that there wasn't too much redesigning to be done. And although everything was new on the A except the suspension and steering, they got very close to hitting their near impossible date.

Prophetically, when Alec Hounslow, who was now in charge of the development department, drove the first prototype, he enthused: 'We'll sell 100,000 of these'. In the end he was only just over 1,000 out; the A sold 101,018.

And amazingly, Lord, who had suddenly started to take notice of the effect racing was having on Jaguar's image and sales, approved of Thornley's plan to launch the A with a three-car team at Le Mans in June 1955.

MG made it to Le Mans with four cars (LBL 301, 302, 303 and 304) that were very close to the production spec. Because the steel production bodies from Pressed Steel had been delayed, though, the three that ran (301, 302 and 303) ran with alloy bodies, as EX182 prototypes. They used 82bhp B-Series engines, tuned by Harry Weslake, and ran with close ratio gearboxes. One car crashed, seriously injuring its driver, Dick Jacobs, the others finished fifth and sixth in their class.

Alongside the huge tragedy of Levegh's Mercedes accident early in the race it seemed of little consequence.

The cars raced again in September, at the Tourist Trophy, and two of the three ran with experimental twin-cam engines, but both retired. That race was again overshadowed by fatal accidents and Lord, more forgivably this time, quickly reverted to his old stance against racing.

September also saw the introduction of the production car, as the MGA, with 1,489cc B-Series engine initially in 68bhp tune, soon with 72bhp. With the more compact B-Series engine, the A had lost its one remaining blemish, the hump in the bonnet, and it was received everywhere as one of the prettiest sports cars in the world.

PAVING THE WAY FOR THE B

The 100mph (160kph) A Roadster that was launched first was joined by a Coupe late in 1956, the Twin-Cam engine (based on the B-Series block) went into production in 1958 and the A sailed onward through its brilliant

Fixed head coupe followed the optional hardtop, and blended remarkably well with the original lines of the open car.

The 100,000th A came out of Abingdon in 1962, just a few months before the B arrived to take up the mantle of MG's people's sports car.

career, paving the way for what inevitably had to be a very special successor.

This time, the timing was a little bit better – though not perfect, because A sales were beginning to fall off quite dramatically by the beginning of the 1960s, from an all-time MG record of over 23,000 cars of all variants in 1959 to a disastrous total of barely 6,000 by 1961.

Nevertheless, at least when the 100,000th A rolled out of Abingdon in March 1962, to the obvious pride of Thornley, Enever and Cecil Cousins who were photographed with

it, they knew that something good was just around the corner.

By this time the B was already well on its way to production, having evolved steadily from the A over the last couple of years, as we shall see shortly, with more than the usual amount of backing. For a short time in the middle of 1962, As and Bs were being built side by side at Abingdon in preparation for the A's phasing out and the B's spectacular introduction. As one classic bowed out, another was all ready to bow in; its development had been another well-kept secret.

3 Developing the B

When MG launched into the project that would become the B, in 1959, there was a lot more to the job than yet another revamping of the theme that had been running since the 1930s with the T-Series cars and through the first 'modern' MG sports car, the A. This time, there was to be a major change in engineering direction too, as MG extended the monocoque construction layout that they had first adopted in 1953 on the ZA Magnette saloon, to their first monocoque sports car.

It would be bringing MG engineering up to date, but it wasn't only an engineering decision. It was commercially and practically ordained, too, by the extent to which the market for MG's sports cars had grown, while the Abingdon works physically couldn't expand.

All MG's sports cars up to the A (and in fact all their cars except the latest Magnette saloons) had used the traditional but labour intensive layout of separate chassis and body units. That layout is technically perfectly sound, but commercially untenable on the scale of production that MG was now reaching. The Magnette had adopted unitary construction because buying-in complete body/chassis units from nearby Pressed Steel allowed a lot more cars to be built (or at least assembled) at Abingdon.

Building a unit construction saloon car (with the inherent strength of a closed structure) is one thing, though – building a unit construction open car is quite another.

INTO NEW TERRITORY

Actually designing a monocoque sports car structure for the B would be new territory for MG, but the B wouldn't be the first monocoque sports car, of course. BMC's little Austin–Healey Sprite (from 1958) and the Sunbeam Alpine (from 1959) were already on the market when planning started for the B, and Abingdon had built both the Sprite and, from June 1961, its MG Midget derivative.

Even so, in addition to the new engineering direction, the putative successor to the A had a lot of other criteria to meet if it was to make its mark in an ever more competitive market. For one thing it had to be at least as quick as the A, and preferably quicker; it had to have all the A's desirable road-holding qualities while losing some of the harsher edges; it had to have better accommodation and trim levels, for a new level of customer (especially in the USA); it had to look good and sell profitably – which meant very big numbers indeed to offset the initially much higher tooling cost of unit construction.

And as important as any of those was that it had to be a real MG . . .

That was what chief engineer Syd Enever, chief chassis draughtsman Roy Brocklehurst, managing director John Thornley and their team set out to achieve with their plans and prototypes for the B; and that, in the end was what they did achieve, although they had to lose some of their more ambitious ideas along the way.

CONVENTIONAL WISDOM

So in the end, unitary or monocoque construction aside, the B was thoroughly conventional, even old-fashioned in many respects, in its basic layout.

John Thornley (left) and Syd Enever, seen here with Stirling
Moss in the EX181 record breaker, were the men behind the B.

As launched, in Roadster form (Tourer in US nomenclature), it was a straightforward, open two-seater with no pretence to any 'plus-two' ability, though there was a modicum of well-trimmed luggage space behind the seats, which could at a pinch be pressed into passenger service. It was smaller than the A in every dimension except width (and weight) but the better packaging that unit construction allowed had given it more passenger space, more luggage space, and more space for added creature comforts. And a new version of the familiar B-Series engine would give it just enough extra power to beat the A's performance figures.

The mechanical layout was still just what Monsieur Panhard had standardised way back in the earliest days of the motor car, with the engine mounted longitudinally at the front and drive going back through a dry-plate clutch and manual gearbox, via the propeller shaft, to a normal rear differential, to drive the rear wheels only. The front was sprung independently, the live rear axle sat on simple semi-elliptic springs, with disc brakes at the front and drums at the rear, plus rack and pinion steering.

All of that changed little in the life of the Roadster, except in details such as the options of overdrive and automatic transmission, a number of wheel and tyre options, some minor suspension revisions and some major engine revisions. The last of those were mainly for the environment-conscious US market, which also caused big changes in the way the B looked, notably with the notorious 'rubber bumpers' of the later models.

In mechanical layout, things changed very little even when the MGB GT joined the family, but a little bit more surgery was required for the GT V8; and a great deal more was required for the six-cylinder MGC – not just in shoehorning the long engine into the nose, but also in changing the more heavily loaded front-suspension from coil springs to

First steps away from the A came with the Frua bodied EX214 styling exercise on the A chassis.

torsion bars, which also gained some much-needed space.

Far from suggesting, though, that the B's engineers were struggling to keep the B afloat, the adaptability of the original layout to four-cylinder and six-cylinder Roadster, and four-, six- and eight-cylinder GT forms, suggests an extraordinary versatility in the basic design.

BACK TO BASICS

Those basics started in the late 1950s, while the A was still enjoying considerable sales success – which was as much a factor in slowing down progress towards the B as was any mechanical or styling consideration. But although BMC certainly weren't profligate with their money when it came to investment in the future, the very nature of MG people was that they were always trying something different.

Even during the lifetime of the A, that had included project EX183, which was a tubular chassised A for Le Mans in 1956; EX186, which was a one-off streamline A racer, with a prototype twin-cam engine and De Dion rear-suspension; EX214, the Frua-bodied A which also reached model form as a fastback and which was a big step towards the B project; and EX216, which was a V4-engined A prototype. There were also fairly regular minor styling change suggestions for the A, including a more forward-sloping nose such as the B would ultimately adopt.

With A sales beginning to slip badly after 1959, though, (from that year's record of well over 23,000 to barely 6,000 by 1961), something more than another minor update was required.

In the end, the B would owe a lot of its styling to one particular MG record breaker, the mid-engined EX181, but the very first ideas for the A's replacement were the roughest of basic outlines sketched by Enever and passed on to apprentice

Frua

Frua, the Torinese styling house which did the earliest (and ultimately rejected) EX214 styling exercises for the B is one of the less glamorous Italian specialists. Founder Pietro Frua worked for several larger studios, including twenty years with Farina, before setting up his own, immediately after World War II.

He began with several small car projects, which included work on the Renault Dauphine, and his first major project for a manufacturer was to design a sports body for that car. That emerged as the Floride, followed by the convertible Caravelle – a car which, ironically perhaps, the B has often been accused of copying. There is also some dispute about whether or not Frua actually designed the Renault on behalf of Ghia.

More glamorously, alongside many smaller projects, Frua styled numerous Maseratis for the 1960s, including the 3500GT, the 5000GT coupe, the beautiful Mistrale and the Quattroporte saloon.

As well as many one-offs in the 1960s, on chassis as diverse as Lotus and Studebaker, Frua designed the whole Glas range of cars for the respected but short-lived German manufacturer.

In 1965 Frua styled the AC 428 (and later the 428 coupe) for what was intended as the Cobra replacement – and Frua also built the steel bodies for those cars, until 1973. After that the company worked mainly on one-offs, but the association with Maserati continued, including cars like the Kyalami in 1979.

draughtsman Peter Neal in the Abingdon design office (which had reopened in its own right, remember, in 1954), to be converted into proper styling drawings. Wooden models were made from Neal's drawings by master model maker Harry Herring, and they were enough to convince the Longbridge hierarchy, in 1957, to commission EX214 – the first Frua-detailed roadster prototype, on an MGA 1500 chassis.

One thing in MG's favour at the time was

*Sleek nose of the EX181 record breaker from 1957 was clearly
instrumental in the eventual shape of the B.*

EX181 at speed on Utah salt flats in 1959.

EX205/1 showed that GT thinking was never far below the surface for Enever and Thornley, but this car was still considered too bulky and weighty: unit construction was the way to go.

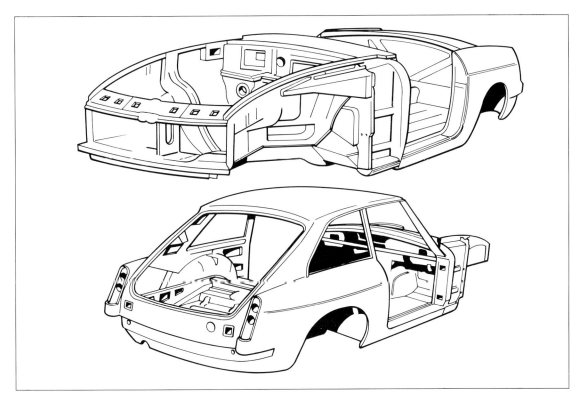

Unitary construction was the B's biggest departure from the A, and worked just as well in either Roadster or GT forms.

that Leonard Lord, BMC's chief executive, was himself something of a compulsive designer, and he was happy to play his part in pursuing the new project.

The Frua car, though, didn't turn out to be a particularly auspicious start, as nobody much liked the uncomfortable mix of Italian and late 1950s American styling, with its heavily chromed front-end treatment and rather Fiat-like side lines. It didn't just look heavy either; it *was* heavy, and that may well have started first thoughts of unit construction as a palliative.

A fastback version of the Frua car, mainly modified by chief body designer John O'Neill and with clear Aston Martin overtones in its roof line, got as far as the model stage, which no doubt confirms that MG were already very keen on building a GT – and managing director John Thornley never made any secret of his admiration for the Aston DB2/4 coupe.

DEVELOPING THE STYLE

Alongside this, O'Neill and chief draughtsman Don Hayter (who had actually come to MG from Aston Martin in 1956) were turning out the first drawings and models in the EX205 series, starting with a quarter-scale model labelled EX205/1.

This car, which was principally Hayter's, obviously drew to a large extent on the EX181 record breaker for its lower body, and the top was just like Hayter's 1960 Le Mans MGA Coupe, but it had a rather uncomfortable front-end treatment – A-like but with a heavy chrome grille. It also had two-tone paint, a fussy, stepped sideline and vestigial rear fins; but on the positive side it had the slightly recessed headlamp treatment that actually did transfer to the B.

That car was the first to be made into a full-size mock-up, being built by Morris Bodies at Coventry in 1958 but bearing the 'number plate' BMC 1959. The grille had been toned down somewhat from the scale model's eggcrate look, and the car was more detailed (with the front side and indicator lamps, for instance), but that was as far as that line of thought went.

What followed, again from Don Hayter, in the form of quarter-scale model EX205/2, was a much neater roadster, on a shorter wheelbase, initially with a grille like that of BMC 1959, but on a slightly stubbier, flatter nose. An early version had twin headlamps, but they were soon dropped in favour of the familiar single, recessed units, while little else changed. At the back, the fins had been toned down (as much for projected ease of production as for aesthetic purposes) and all in all (grille apart) this single headlamp car looked as close to the B as makes little difference.

From it, Hayter went straight into a series of EX214/– variants, similar styles but with different engine options, the drawings all being completed in mid-1958. A large part of what Hayter had to do at this stage was to pare down the size of the new car, and his largely competition-based background obviously helped with that – in fact the B was one of his first 'non-competition' jobs.

THE ENGINE OPTIONS

The variants he drew included such possibilities as a proposed V4, the MGA Twin Cam unit, and a four-cylinder modification of the existing six-cylinder C-Series engine (as introduced in 1954).

The chopped C-Series would seem to have been the first choice of power unit for the new car, but the number of variations drawn around the V4 suggest that that was a very serious possibility at the time (and it could also have translated into an easily accommodated V6 variant at some time in the future, of course).

The V4 possibility, a 60 degree unit with a

Clean, uncluttered lines of the original B Roadster with its 'traditional' MG radiator grille and very little superfluous brightwork were arguably never bettered in the car's long production life – though many a late-model owner would no doubt argue the point.

Model: MGB MkI   **Years:** 1962–1967

Body type: Two-seat open tourer, unitary construction
Engine type: Four-cylinder, in-line
Capacity: 1,798cc
Bore: 80.3mm
Stroke: 88.9mm
Compression ratio: 8.8:1
Cylinders: Cast-iron block, five main bearings (three bearings up to 1964)
Cylinder head: Cast-iron, two valves per cylinder operated by pushrods
Fuel system: Twin SU carburettors
Maximum power: 95bhp @ 5,400rpm
Maximum torque: 110lb ft @ 3,000rpm
Bhp per litre: 52.8
Gearbox type: Four-speed manual (overdrive optional from 1963)
Gear ratios: Top: 1.00   2nd: 2.21   Reverse: 4.75
                3rd: 1.37   1st: 3.63
Final drive ratio: 3.90:1
Clutch: Single dry plate, hydraulic operation
Front-suspension: Independent, by double wishbones, coil springs, lever arm
                dampers, optional anti-roll bar
Rear-suspension: Live axle, semi-elliptic leaf springs, lever arm dampers
Brakes: Solid front discs, rear drums
Steering: Rack and pinion
Wheels & tyres: 4J×14in steel discs (4.5J×14in wires optional); 5.60×14in tyres
Overall length: 153.3in
Overall width: 59.7in
Overall height: 49.4in
Wheelbase: 91.0in
Track: Front: 49.0in   Rear: 49.3in
Ground clearance: 4.5in
Fuel tank capacity: 10 gallons (12 gallons from 1965)
Unladen weight: 2,050lb
Power to weight ratio: 103.8bhp/ton

PERFORMANCE

Maximum speed: 103mph
0–60mph: 12.2 seconds
Standing ¼ mile: 18.5 seconds
Fuel consumption: 27mpg

single central cam and complex valvegear, also accounts for the B's wide bonnet line, which appeared right from the earliest styling stages. MG had learned with the A that the narrow bonnet virtually ruled out the V option, even if the engine was very short; in the B, the wide cover even allowed the V8 at a later stage.

Two, possibly three cars *were* built with V4 engines, according to Roy Brocklehurst, but it was a blind alley. Predictably enough, the V4/V6 series was cancelled for economical and internal political reasons (although there were technical problems too, including difficulties in balancing the engines properly). The 'four-cylinder C-Series' was never developed, the 1,588cc Twin Cam's dreadful lack of reliability ruled that one out, and MG were forced back to the old corporate parts bin. That, in the end, meant the B-Series, but all that was for the future. First the car had to get the go-ahead.

NEXT STEPS

The model for board approval was quickly built from the drawings, and almost immediately turned into a full-scale mock-up, which was the final step to the B – the basic design quickly being given the AD023 project number which showed that it was now destined for production.

It took almost exactly two years to get from basic approval of AD023, in 1958, to the appearance of the first fully engineered B prototype in mid-1960, and there was still a long way to go from there to production, including a major rethink of the rear-suspension layout and the adoption of a new version of the B-Series engine. And, of course, there was also a tremendous amount of detail work to be done on furniture and fittings, on making the design work in production terms, on testing and on costing.

Once the basic engine type had been finalised, the most important running change during development from prototype to production was to the rear-suspension.

Originally, thought was given to an independent rear-suspension to go with the independent front, but with live axles being built in such huge numbers at the Drews Lane Tractors and Transmissions plant, that didn't progress beyond drawings. A live axle layout, but using coil springs instead of the familiar semi-elliptic 'cart' springs, was then tried on a modified MGA chassis.

This layout used trailing radius arms for fore and aft location, and originally had an effective but expensive Watts linkage for lateral location. The idea was to design a system which would have given scope for longer suspension movement with softer spring rates, and therefore better ride qualities than the rather harsh A.

Brocklehurst managed to survive turning over and writing off a test-bed A fitted with the trailing arm type of suspension, while out on test near the Abingdon factory, but that was all in a day's work . . .

By the time the first true B prototype was built (in mid-1960 at Morris Bodies with final assembly at Abingdon), the Watts linkage had been swapped for a cheaper Panhard rod.

Unfortunately, this didn't really do the job either, presenting problems with mounting point breakages and then with rear-end steering, and given that the project was already falling behind schedule for the originally proposed late 1961 launch, it was decided to go back to the old faithful leaf springs.

Given the amount of work that Enever in particular had done (on new interleaving materials, for example, for cutting down noise, wear and friction), they still weren't a bad solution at the time.

ALMOST THERE

In other respects, the car was getting pretty close to the production look, but with some

The interior gained a considerable amount of space and creature comfort over the A, but MG resisted the temptation to try and squeeze in a real rear seat – at least until the GT arrived.

noticeable detail differences. There was a slightly slimmer windscreen frame, for instance, though already with the centre strut for the interior mirror; the front sidelights were pinched, temporarily, from the Triumph Herald; the rear lights had separate rather than integral reflectors; there were no rear overriders, and therefore a different rear number plate and light arrangement; there was a fiddly trim moulding along the top edges of the sills below the doors; and there was a metal tonneau over the space behind the front seats.

Inside, this first prototype (which was right-hand drive) had a fairly basic dashboard which was originally intended for a later A but which isn't dissimilar from a real B's; it still had an A steering wheel; the handbrake was straight rather than kinked, and in chrome; the gearlever had no surround, just a simple rubber gaiter through the carpet; and the door trims were pretty basic.

There were other mechanical differences, too. The engine was the 1,588cc B-Series from the 'Mk I' A, with pancake air filters rather than the slightly more efficient Coopers paper element ones that the B eventually adopted (the 1,622cc engine hadn't even appeared in the production A by this

B-series engine for the B gained more than originally intended in capacity to offset weight, but started its run with a three-bearing crank – soon changed to the stronger five-bearing type.

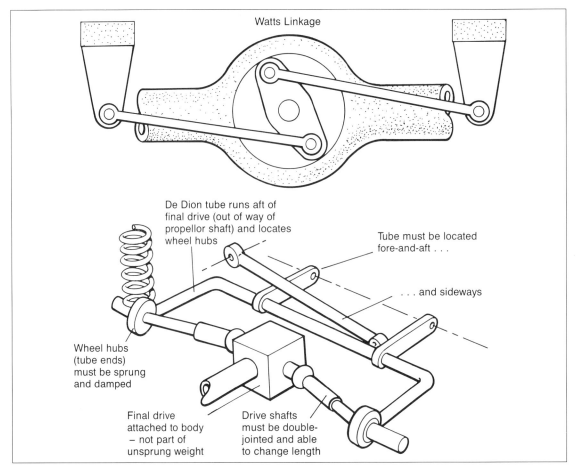

Watts Linkage

De Dion tube runs aft of
final drive (out of way of
propellor shaft) and locates
wheel hubs

Tube must be located
fore-and-aft . . .

. . . and sideways

Wheel hubs
(tube ends)
must be sprung
and damped

Final drive
attached to body
– not part of
unsprung weight

Drive shafts
must be double-
jointed and able
to change length

Among suspension options tried on the rear of the car during
development were Watts linkage and De Dion, but cheap and
cheerful cart springs prevailed.

stage, that didn't happen until June 1961);
there was no oil cooler with the smaller
engine; and the independent front-
suspension crossmember was welded rather
than bolted to the shell.

The cart-sprung rear axle layout of the A
re-appeared on the second and third B prototypes, which were built more or less simultaneously in mid-1961 – again with the
1,588cc engines as the then-planned 1,622cc
unit *still* wasn't available.

Because the springs had to be longer for the
B than they had been on the A, the rear of the
car had to be lengthened by a full inch over
the first B prototype, with considerable
modification around the boot floor area in

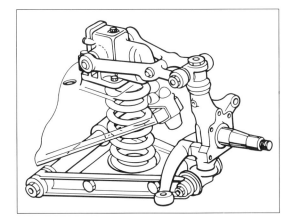

Independent front suspension dated
back in essence to the Y-type saloon,
but it was ideal for its role on the B.

Syd Enever

Albert Sydney 'Syd' Enever, the man who created the MGA and the MGB as well as the staggeringly successful pre-war and post-war MG record breakers, was involved with MG all his working life.

He was born in March 1906 at Colden Common in Hampshire, but as a child moved back to his mother's native Oxford when his parents split up. He was educated at South Oxford School and went straight from there to a job as messenger boy with the Morris Garages – in 1920, even before Cecil Kimber arrived and several years before MG evolved.

In 1927 Kimber recognised his mechanical aptitudes and took him into the fledgling MG experimental department under Cec Cousins – who actually *was* MG's first employee. In 1929, Enever became chief experimental engineer and from then on he was closely involved in every MG up to and including the B GT V8, which was his last production project.

Alongside the production cars, Enever (working closely with Reg Jackson) developed a whole series of MG record cars which gave no-one else a look-in in the 1,100cc Class F and 1,500cc Class E categories both before and after World War II. And for all his outstanding achievements with MG production cars, those, justifiably, were always the cars that Enever was most proud of.

He stayed at Abingdon even after the Morris takeover in 1935, when almost everyone else was moved to Cowley, and was head of the experimental department until 1938. As chief planning engineer he worked on developing the Crusader tank during the war, resuming his role in the experimental department from 1946 to 1954.

From 1954 until his retirement in 1971 he was MG's chief engineer, a Member of the Fellowship of the Motor Industry, and with John Thornley he shaped the whole modern face of the MG marque – especially in the guise of the MGA and MGB.

His racing and record breaking background was never far away from the road cars either; the A developed directly from the specially bodied George Phillips Le Mans racers and the B owed a great deal to the streamliners. As Enever himself once said: 'The MGB shape, though you might not realise it, was basically borrowed from EX181.'

His last production project was the V8, and one of the last jobs he was involved with at Abingdon was the mid-engined ADO21; when he retired in 1971, just a couple of years after John Thornley, MG (and indeed BL) lost one of their finest assets. Syd died in 1993.

order to incorporate the revised mountings. This meant that the spare wheel could be laid flat rather than angled into a well as it was on the first prototype, and there were no longer any turrets intruding into the boot, inboard of the wheelarches, for the spring/damper units of the coil spring layout.

These later prototypes used alloy boot, door and bonnet skins, as the engineers would have liked to have done for production, but given cost and manufacturing constraints only the alloy bonnet survived – and that only until 1970.

They were also used for finalising the body details for Pressed Steel, and for completing designs for interior and exterior trim detailing – and also including two different types of hood, a detachable one and a folding one.

And finally, the prototypes were used for driving evaluation, much of it at Chalgrove airfield, which was conveniently near the Abingdon works. The main problem that that revealed was one of scuttle shake, which resulted in the car receiving some reinforcing behind the facia.

As well as the development testing, there were also facilities at Abingdon for doing destructive testing such as barrier impacts and roll-overs.

One of the 'might-have-beens': the front-drive AD034 prototype from 1960 followed corporate thinking but wasn't popular with front-drive pioneer Issigonis.

PREPARING FOR PRODUCTION

After the first three prototypes, MG built a series of eight pre-production cars, whose joint roles were to iron out final design details and to allow a build familiarisation programme. These cars were also built in 1961 and included both left- and right-hand drive versions.

The change from the planned 1,622cc engine to the 1,798cc unit which essentially saw the B right through its production life was taken at a very late stage. The MG engineers already knew that the B had turned out to be heavier than they had expected, and as a result was worryingly slower than the final As. The 1,798cc unit arrived fortuitously via the forthcoming front-drive Austin 1800, which was due to appear in 1964 with this capacity.

While the engineering details for the B were being finalised, so were some of the commercial ones, and the crux of those was the agreement between MG and Pressed Steel for the body/chassis units. By 1965, Pressed Steel had been absorbed into the BMC empire, but the company was still negotiating contracts just like any other customer.

Without a neat piece of wheeling and dealing from John Thornley, the B project might have stopped here, but MG people are cleverer than that. Faced with an initial tooling cost that he realised was way beyond what he could get past the corporate beancounters, Thornley talked Pressed Steel into a lower initial cost plus a higher price per unit delivered, and the B became the first complete car that Pressed Steel worked on at their new Swindon plant.

In the long term, Pressed Steel did very nicely out of the deal, as B production ran on and on; without it, the B wouldn't have happened at all. But thanks to Thornley sticking his neck out it did, and the launch was approaching rapidly . . .

4 Into Production

The big day was 20 September 1962, when the B was officially unveiled at the press preview for the London Motor Show in Earls Court.

Looking back at the motoring media for some time prior to the actual unveiling, it is fairly clear that the B was news to most people. Even the MG magazine *Safety Fast* didn't make any allusions to the B before it appeared, and that month's Editorial began: 'Rumours about a new MG sports car to succeed the "MGA" have been flying for quite a while; some have been wildly astray while others have been embarassingly near the mark . . .'

In 1962, of course, artist's impressions and spy photographs were not the sort of staple diet that they are nowadays. Even in the May 1962 edition of *Safety Fast*, when the 100,000th A was celebrated, there was no mention of a possible successor.

But the B was, of course, splashed across the cover of the October edition, above the cover line: 'Two Brand-New MGs – Full Details Inside'.

The other new MG was the front-drive MG 1100 saloon – a badge engineered Issigonis 1100, but advertised by BMC as 'the most advanced MG ever'. It was a good car, and it was by no means unlikely that the next MG sports car would have front-wheel drive too, and Hydrolastic suspension, but for the moment the conventional soft-top, two-seater B was what MG enthusiasts really wanted to see.

The line inside *Safety Fast* read: 'This month's cover: Formula for fun! – sunshine, a pretty girl and a brand new sports car that sets new standards in comfort and effortless performance – it's the new MG Series MGB'.

The full-page BMC advertisement on the inside front cover also underlined the selling points of the new B: 'The new, SUPERLATIVE MGB, with 1,800cc engine'. The big copy splash said: 'MORE POWER! – 1,800cc engine, Disc brakes on front wheels'.

But the real message was in the smaller print, which talked of: 'Twin carburetters with twin air cleaners and silencers. Independent front suspension, 94bhp at 5,500rpm. Direct rack and pinion steering giving finger-tip control, new type diaphragm spring clutch, mono-construction steel body. Wrap-around windscreen, *Extra roomy* cockpit – more room for occasional passenger'.

And it finished with the obvious exhortation: 'EVERYTHING FOR *SAFETY FAST* MG MOTORING'.

The italics on '*Extra roomy*' showed that BMC knew what they were selling; the immediate rush of orders suggested that enthusiasts knew what they were buying; and with production having been under way since June of that year the B was available from stock for immediate delivery – especially to the all-important US market.

The Show was quite a big occasion for MG, with the new 1100 saloon and new 1100 engines for the Midget sharing the limelight, but the big rush was for the bigger sports car.

THE BONES OF THE B

There was a complete B on the stand, and there was another half a B (split down the middle) to show just how different the car was from the A.

What it revealed was a handsomely styled,

*B-Day was 20 September 1962 and the B Roadster shared its
show debut with the front-drive MG 1100 saloon.*

Although the B had considerably more luggage space than the A, the boot rack was always a popular addition.

if essentially conventional, front-engined rear-drive two-seater, but with a unitary construction body and quite a few other refinements.

The new Pressed Steel built body/chassis unit was the B's big departure, of course. Essentially, it comprises a flat floorpan with a central transmission tunnel (joined by a box section to the front bulkhead), box-section side members (the outside of which are the sills), and a box-section crossmember running across the car below the seat position. The side members continue backwards,

up and over the rear axle to act as the rear spring hangers, and forwards to form the engine bearers and the front-suspension carrying rails.

You couldn't help noticing, either, that there was a lot of room around the B-Series engine under the wide bonnet – especially ahead of it towards the radiator, where there might easily have been room for a couple of extra cylinders . . .

A double-front transverse bulkhead and the inner wing panels rising from the engine-bearing rails form a rigid front bay to accept both engine and front-suspension loads, completed at their front end by the diaphragm on which the radiator is mounted, and by the flat, horizontal panel above and behind the front valance. The rear bulkhead, boot floor and inner wing panels do a similar job for the rear-suspensions loads, leaving the majority of the outer bodywork essentially unstressed – although the steel skinned doors do add considerable strength to the monocoque, and on US models incorporate side-intrusion protection.

The front wings bolt on, the rear wings are welded on, and the mounts for the substantial alloy windscreen frame attach to the inside of the shell below the dash, with just two bolts.

At the rear, the live axle (initially the 'banjo' type carried over from the A) sits on those semi-elliptic leaf springs; at the front, the suspension, mounted on a detachable subframe, with rubber bushes for noise insulation, is independent, by upper and lower wishbones and coil springs. There are lever type Armstrong hydraulic dampers on both front and rear, and rack and pinion steering, just as on the A; the only real difference between the two set-ups is that the B is considerably softer all round than the uncompromisingly sporty A.

MG kept the 'office' simple but functional, but the B scored over the A with wind-up windows, external door locks and even a lockable glovebox.

Press release photographs described carpeted ledge as an 'occasional' rear seat. The hole in the tunnel is for optional seat belts – not then compulsory.

INDEPENDENT ORIGINS

Although both ends *are* essentially the same as the on the A, their origins stretch back well beyond that. Even the independent front is virtually identical to that designed by Alec Issigonis and former MG draughtsman Jack Daniels (who also collaborated on the Morris Minor) for the pre-war Morris Ten saloon. It never appeared on the Morris, simply for reasons of cost, but Syd Enever quickly picked it up for MG, in 1939.

It should still have appeared before the war, on a car which (in spite of an Abingdon prototype number, EX166) was actually designed in Coventry – and would have been the first MG not designed by Kimber. That was the MG Ten, intended for unveiling at the 1940 Motor Show as a 1941 model.

With more pressing problems to be overcome, there weren't many 1941 models of any kind around Europe, of course, so when the Y-Type saloon appeared in 1947, there it was – one of the first independent front suspensions on a British production car.

The Y also used rack and pinion steering (the first Nuffield car to do so), and in 1949 the TD (Enever's first complete road car project, with MG stalwart Cec Cousins) adopted both.

The TD was a milestone car for MG. The TC (which later found its way into the New York Museum of Moderns Art's exhibition 'Eight Automobiles' as the definitive European sports car) had been the advance party into the USA, the TD was the main invasion. It was the first MG to offer left-hand drive from the works, it consciously offered more comfort than the TC (just as the B would over the A) and around eighty per cent of production eventually went to the USA.

The fact that the suspension carried on through the TD, the TF and the A right into the B isn't entirely due to BMC parsimony, it actually was a very good layout. It is very compact, for one thing, and mounts to the car as a complete unit on the massive crossmember.

On each side, the inner ends of the lower wishbone are rubber bushed (to isolate road noise) and pivot on a long pin through the crossmember. At its outer end, the wishbone is attached by another pin to the bottom of the kingpin. The inner end of the top wishbone attaches via a pivoting top link to the top of the kingpin, and that top wishbone is actually the arms of the Armstrong double-acting lever-type damper, which is mounted on top of the crossmember.

The stub axle casting fits around the kingpin between upper and lower wishbones and the steering arms extend from it, connecting to the steering tie rods via ball joints.

The coil spring which is the load carrier is sandwiched between a plate on the lower wishbone at its bottom end, and the under-

*This beautifully-maintained example shows off the classic lines
of the B.*

side of the crossmember (directly below the damper body) at its top end. The type of front hub, of course, depends on the type of wheel fitted – a four-stud plate for steel disc wheels or a splined centre-lock type for knock-on wire wheels.

On cars with the initially optional but later standard front anti-roll bar, the cranked transverse bar runs in bearings which are attached directly to the body shell and pick up onto the lower wishbones through a vertical link.

The steering rack is also mounted directly to the crossmember, with four bolts, which makes the whole assembly even more attractively compact – and, of course, very easy to remove for maintenance once the steering column and brake lines are disconnected. On most cars, the precise rack and pinion steering requires only three turns from lock to lock, but in 1976 a slower rack was adopted which needed three and a half turns, making the car feel slightly less sharp than before.

At the rear, the semi-elliptic springs had five leaves plus a bottom plate (or six plus a bottom plate on later cars) and also used Armstrong dampers. There were substantial bump stop rubbers above the rear axle to cope with major potholes, and a rebound strap to cope with sudden bumps.

Like the A, the B used Lockheed disc brakes at the front, but as the road wheel diameter had gone down from 15in (38cm) to 14in (35cm), the discs were slightly smaller too, at 10.75in (27cm) rather than a full 11in (28cm). The rear drums, on the other hand, were identical to those on the A, of 10in (25cm) diameter.

The engine *had* changed from TF to A, with the introduction (post BMC merger) of the less lofty (physically, not philosophically) Austin-sourced B-Series allowing the production A to adopt a smooth bonnet where the T-Series based EX175 prototype had had a bulge to accommodate the tall XPAG engine. It did change, too, between the A and the B – but only in capacity, not in type.

THE B FOR THE B

The four-cylinder, pushrod overhead-valve B-Series engine was introduced to BMC as a modified Austin engine in 1953, with the option of various capacities from 1,200cc upwards, but all based on a stroke of 88.9mm.

That stroke figure (which is a comfortable 3.5in in imperial units), and the basic bottom-end layout that goes with it, are traceable back to the Austin 10 engine of 1932.

The 10, of course, was a side-valve engine, and the top end of the B-Series essentially stems from a totally different engine line, Austin's first ever overhead-valve unit – a 3.5-litre, six-cylinder truck engine introduced in 1939.

The early layout of side-cam, with carbs and manifolds on one side, ignition and dynamo electrics on the other, set the pattern for the later A-, B- and C-Series BMC engines, while much of the work on the new cylinder head was done by 'freelance' genius Harry Weslake – pioneer of scientific gas flowing in cylinder head design.

From trucks, the six progressed to the big post-war Austin saloons, the Sheerline and the Princess; and during World War II Austin developed a long-stroke four-cylinder 2.2-litre overhead-valve engine based on the six. That engine developed through the early post-war mid-sized Austin A40 saloons like the Devon, Dorset and Somerset, in which it was reduced to 1.2 litres, but still with a proportionally long stroke.

They were the last Austin engines so encumbered, because the archaic and arcane British taxation system which had long encouraged long-stroke designs (simultaneously *discouraging* a lot of better options) was finally dropped in January 1948 – largely as a result of well-presented arguments against them from Nuffield's Miles Thomas. It's interesting to note, though, that Austin's sense of adventure didn't stretch to trying oversquare (or even quite square)

*B underbonnet layout is neat and accessible, but the heater unit
(to left of picture) was only an option on early cars. This is a
left-hand drive export model.*

dimensions and losing the torquey, 'slogging' nature of the long-stroke configuration altogether.

The stroke of the late 1940s A40 engine mentioned above was in fact 3.5in (88.9mm) too, and as such, that engine shared the same dimensions as the smallest of all the real B-Series engines, the 1,200cc unit that appeared in the Cambridge-type A40 (and the Morris Cowley) in 1954; but the dimension was coincidental, and it was *not* a B-Series engine.

The real B-Series, designed almost in its entirety by Eric Bareham, had an enormous number of detail (but fundamental) differences – not least of them the scope for expanding to usefully larger capacities.

In fact, between Austin's very first thoughts for the B-Series and the engine actually appearing, the Austin/Morris merger into BMC had taken place (in November 1951), so the B-Series effectively became the first 'corporate' engine – and far and away the most versatile one.

And the first car ever to appear with the B-Series engine wasn't an Austin or a Morris, but an MG; the ZA series Magnette (which also, of course, introduced unit construction to the marque).

That was in October 1953, at the London

Substantial alloy windscreen frame contributes considerably to chunky look of the Roadster and was changed from early prototypes.

Motor Show, and the B-Series appeared as a 60bhp, 1,489cc unit — in which capacity it also first found its way into the MGA 1500 Roadster in October 1955, with 68bhp (soon raised to 72) at 5,500rpm. In this guise the engine had larger valves, double valve springs, a higher compression ratio and

Neat pop-studs are for rear tonneau and hood fixing.

modified pistons, and seen alongside the basic 42bhp 1,200cc engine it said a lot about the inherent versatility of the design.

POWER OFF THE SHELF

It is probably fair to say that without the availability of the B-Series, 'off-the-shelf', the MGA wouldn't have happened at all (BMC had taken a long time to make their minds up about it, with the issue confused by the launch of the Austin–Healey 100 which conveniently used up otherwise redundant Austin engines); and if the A hadn't happened, the B certainly wouldn't have.

From July 1959, capacity was up to 1,588cc for the MGA 1600 (and power to 79bhp at 5,600rpm). And the final upgrading for the A (notwithstanding the B-Series based Twin-Cam) was to 1,622cc and 86bhp at 5,500rpm for the 1600 MkII in June 1962 — in which guise the engine was originally intended for the forthcoming B, too.

As eventually used in the B, though, its capacity had gone up to its final production stretch, at 1,798cc — a capacity which would have been thought impossible from the B-Series only a few years earlier.

The capacity increase came from an increase in bore, from 76.2 to 80.26mm (exactly 3in to 3.16in) while the stroke stayed at the ubiquitous 88.9mm (3.5in) just like every other B-Series before it and after. That figure *couldn't* be increased because of the proximity of the crank throws to the camshaft position in the side of the block, but the crank bearing diameters were increased from 2in (5cm) to 2.125in (5.4cm) and the crank webs were made slightly thicker.

To achieve the bigger bores, the engineers had had to lose virtually all the metal in the centre of the block, siamesing the bores and leaving only a small water passage between the two central ones. That was only made possible by improved casting techniques, but

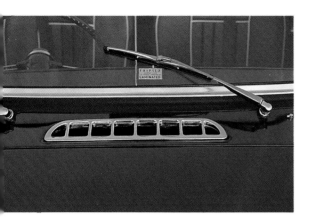

The neat heater vent is ahead of the windscreen, and the B was a major advance over the A in having both external door handles and locks.

it was totally successful in production and never gave any problems.

The new 1,798cc engine, even though it still had only three main bearings, was stronger than the 1,622cc type, smoother running and with a better torque curve.

There was even one further stretch to the B's capacity from the works, to just over 2 litres, but that was strictly for racing only and is described in our racing chapters. As described later, the only fundamental change to the B-Series throughout its life in the B (aside from emissions-related equipment) was the change from three main bearings to five, in October 1964.

Don Hayter

Don Hayter, the man who styled the B, was born in 1927, and when he left school in 1942 he went straight to Pressed Steel, in Coventry — the company which eventually built the B body shells. In 1942, Pressed Steel were engaged in war work, of course, producing large aircraft assemblies. Don Hayter worked in the drawing office, turning design drawings into production drawings.

When the war finished and Pressed Steel returned to automotive work, Hayter continued to do the same, often complex job for cars including the Jaguar XK120 and the MG Magnette.

In 1954 he moved to Aston Martin, as a draughtsman, but when Aston moved from Feltham to Newport Pagnell, he left and early in 1956 found himself at Abingdon, as chief body draughtsman (alongside Brocklehurst as chief chassis draughtsman). His earliest work was on the A Twin Cam, and he also did the Ted Lund racing A coupe for Le Mans. Not long after that, he started work on the EX205 series that pre-dated the B, and then on the EX214/– designs that were the final stage.

Once the B got the go-ahead, it was largely Hayter's job to make it buildable, and he also finalised the dash design, the distinctive windscreen and the hood. He also had to redesign the rear end at a late stage when the cart-spring rear-suspension was adopted in preference to the more complex systems that had been rejected.

Hayter took over the development department in 1968, and among other projects he worked on the SSV-1 safety car (based on the B GT), the mid-engined AD021 prototype and on the shell of the lightweight MGC GT racer, the GTS.

When Roy Brocklehurst left MG in July 1973, Don Hayter succeeded him as chief engineer. In that capacity, he was deeply involved in all MG's (and much of BL's) US safety legislation work, including the B's switch to rubber bumpers.

Come 1980 and the closure of Abingdon, Don Hayter was one of the very last people to leave the old works.

THE WEIGHT PROBLEM

In fact the B-Series stretch had been made for the forthcoming Austin 1800 front-drive saloon (which, along with the later Princess was the only other car ever to use the engine in 1,798cc guise) rather than for the MGB itself, but the B was the first to use it – and it couldn't have been better timed.

The car *had* turned out to be overweight, around 50lb heavier than the final A, and with the 1,622cc, 86bhp 1600 MkII A engine it was obviously slightly slower than its predecessor, which would have been rather embarrassing.

The 1,798cc engine, running on an 8.8:1 compression ratio (using slightly dish-topped pistons to compensate for the bigger capacity) and two SU H4 carburetters, gave a useful increase in power, to 95bhp at 5,500rpm.

Its cylinder head was very similar to that on the A (and on most other B-Series engines), having Weslake's familiar, heart-shaped combustion chambers and inlet and exhaust ports on the same side, with vertical valves operated by pushrods and rockers. The exhausts have separate ports for the outer cylinders, siamesed ones for the middle cylinders – which give the engine as used in

Steel disc wheels were standard equipment from the launch, as was the detachable-type hood. Left-hand drive and whitewall tyres are among few visual distinguishing features of the export car.

the B one of its few common faults, a tendency to 'run-on' when very hot. The inlets use two pairs of siamesed ports.

With its relatively long stroke, it was another impressively torquey engine, that peak going up from the A's 97lb ft at 4,000rpm to 110lb ft at only 3,000 – making it a willing slogger.

The four-speed manual gearbox was identical to that in the A except that it had a lower first gear ratio, and a direct change where the A had needed a remote linkage because the driver sat further back from the engine/gearbox.

With this gearbox and the 1,798cc engine's new urge, honour was restored, and the B was respectably quicker than the A.

Autocar's first test of the B, in October 1962, managed 103mph (165kph) and 0–60mph (0–96.5kph) in 12.2 seconds. *Motor* didn't get their hands on the B until a couple of weeks later and then recorded 108mph (173kph) and 0–60mph (0–96.5kph) in 12.1 seconds. *Autosport* tried the same car as both the others (523 CBL) in December, and with the talents of John Bolster and possibly just a little loosening up of the engine by then, managed a remarkable 109.5mph (176kph) and 0–60mph (0–96.5kph) in only 11.4 seconds – which is probably the best set of figures anybody ever saw for the car.

Bolster started his test with the words:

'The world of the sports car is changing fast. We used to admire the type of two-seater that was all engine and performance and precious little else. Most people still imagine that they would like this sort of machine, but when it comes to signing a cheque they always go for something less spartan. A sports car must still have superior performance and handling qualities but it is now expected to have all the creature comforts of a luxurious saloon, which means that noise, vibration, and hard suspension are out.

'Such a car is the MGB . . .'

Bolster went on to like most of what he found in the new car, from the newfound trim refinement (including the 'controversial' wind-up windows), through the extra luggage space both behind the seats and in the boot, to the car's flexibility, performance and road manners.

Like almost everyone else who commented on the car, he was obviously especially taken by its looks, too.

A PROMISING START

In all of that, he was not alone; the B was well received in virtually all quarters, and Bernard Cahier, writing in the American magazine *Sports Car Graphic* in November 1962, concluded: 'Let's face it: it is the best MG yet made. I truly enjoyed driving it, being particularly impressed by its new design, refined features, general performance and handling . . .'

As for the rest of the creature comforts that MG were pleased to note, the B was a big advance on the A in almost every respect.

In spite of being three inches shorter in the wheelbase (at 91in (231cm)) and almost three inches shorter overall (at 153.2in (389cm)), the B was far roomier inside than the A, and had substantially more luggage capacity. It was a touch wider (by a couple of inches, at just a fraction under five feet), which immediately gave a bit more seat and shoulder space, but other benefits were felt all round.

Much of the newfound space, of course, came from the better packaging allowed by the unitary construction shell. By setting the front bulkhead and footwells well forward, the B allowed its newly designed seats to be fully six inches further forward than on the A, improving the leg room while still allowing the 'occasional' passenger/luggage space behind the seats – where the A's pushed right up to the rear bulkhead.

And because the seats were low-mounted (and the ground clearance was a couple of

inches lower), there was adequate headroom when the hood was up, even for taller drivers. The seats were adjustable for rake, but only if you took a spanner to the nut on the base of the back.

The boot was usefully larger too, because the tail didn't fall away so sharply and it wasn't so constrained by structural bits and pieces. In fact the A's boot was little more than token, while the B's – even when partly filled with such essentials as spare wheel, jack, tools and optional folding hood– actually offered some worthwhile space.

There was a glovebox in the dash for oddments, too; and it locked! Even the doors didn't do that on the A Roadster with its internal handles.

And as well as lockable glovebox, doors and boot, (with external handles) the B even had wind-up windows – which, amazingly it seems now, were a cause of some controversy among 'traditionalists' at the time.

The American magazine *Car and Driver* subsequently summed up the feel of the B quite nicely in their December 1964 test, which included the lovely summation: 'It is particularly pleasant to note the absence of walnut trim on the dash and in its place a black crackle finish. Most British manufacturers of small cars cling to the notion that a few square inches of wood glued to the dash smacks of so much overt luxury that the passengers will forget they are not riding in a Bentley Continental . . .' And, later: 'There is an atmosphere that permeates the car that says "MG". No enthusiast can climb into the machine without being instantly aware that this is an MG . . .'

Finally, as well as the new passive comforts, every tester was quick to remark on the B's new dynamic refinements: they liked the more powerful but less stressed engine with its well chosen gear ratios; they liked the comfortable leather-trimmed seats, the relaxed driving position, and the pleasant lack of wind noise at high speeds; they liked the softer but still well damped ride and the predictable, grippy road-holding; and while most of them did say that the character had changed a great deal from the A, they were quite happy to welcome the B as a real MG.

INSTANT SUCCESS

So although there were already some small asides from other directions to the effect that it was maybe already a little old-fashioned under the new unitary skin, it's unlikely that MG lost much sleep over them. From Day One they could sell the B as quickly as they could build it; if they had any regrets at all it must have been that the B eventually arrived rather later than they originally intended – having been planned first for late 1961, which soon slipped to early 1962 and finally the September date.

As launched at Earls Court, the B Roadster was listed in Britain at £690 plus forty-five per cent purchase tax, which brought that up to £949.15.3d. At least it did until November, when the tax was reduced to twenty-five per cent – fortuitously bringing the basic B down to just £834.6s.

That would get you on the road with a basic car standing on steel wheels (which both Enever and Thornley always preferred to wire ones which they thought faddy and out-dated), with a rather fiddly detachable hood, no heater, no radio, no nothing much in fact, other than fresh air MG motoring.

Wire wheels are an attractive option frowned on by both Enever and Thornley as essentially anachronistic.

The Sunbeam Alpine beat the B into production with 'unitary' chassis, from 1959, competing on price but not performance.

On top of that, you *could* add wire wheels (slightly wider than the 4J steel ones, at 4½J) for an extra £34.7.6d, a 'De Luxe' fixed folding hood (which folded down into the space behind the seats) in a choice of colours for £5.10s, a tonneau cover (standard on export cars) for £11, the heater for £16.17s, and the oil cooler that MG had deemed necessary as standard on export models as an £18.19s extra on domestic market cars. Even the ashtray that perched on the transmission tunnel ahead of the gearlever was an extra, listed at £1.7.6d. A radio, for which there was space in the centre of the dash, with an octagonal speaker fitting above the transmission tunnel, was a matter of choice, but the standard offering was a Radiomobile set.

A COMPETITIVE OFFERING

Even loaded up with all the goodies, the B was very competitively priced against the contemporary opposition.

In 1962 that included, principally, the Sunbeam Alpine, the Triumph TR4 and the Austin-Healey 3000 – plus a small list of more obscure options which were more 'paper' competitors than commercial ones.

The Sunbeam, launched in 1959, was the nearest thing to the B on price, at £956 alongside the B's launch price of £949. That was with the initially higher purchase tax – although when that went down, it went down for everyone, of course.

The Sunbeam was close to the B in other ways too. It was comfortable and well equipped for instance, and to a degree it was the kind of car that had obliged MG to add some of the creature comforts that it had to the B.

The Alpine was not desperately sophisticated on the mechanical side, however; although it had unit construction, it was based on the short-wheelbase Husky estate car floorpan and was markedly heavier than the B, which kept performance significantly adrift of the MG's. With 80bhp from its 1,592cc engine in 1962 models it was struggling to reach 100mph (160kph), and 0–60mph (0–96.5kph) was up in the 14-second region.

In truth, the Alpine never really aspired to the real sporting feel of the B either, or even of the B's other closest competitor, the TR4.

With 2.1 litres and 100bhp, the Triumph was pretty well on a par with the B for performance (in spite of being heavier – again largely thanks to a separate chassis). Typical figures for the TR were a 102mph (164kph) maximum and 11 seconds for 0–60mph (0–96.5kph). Its other advantage was that it had beaten the B into production by a year just at the time when the A was having to struggle. In the USA it was really the *only* serious opposition for the B, but all that was only relative, as B sales were always comfortably superior.

The B's ride and handling were superior too, at least until the TR4 gained independent rear-suspension, in 1965 as the TR4A; but by then it didn't matter much in terms of volume sales, the B was a runaway winner.

The other major drawback for the TR was that it cost £1,030 when the B appeared, and cost was a very important factor in the early 1960s.

The big Healey was even more, of course, at £1,190 – and if a difference of around £240 sounds rather insignificant in today's terms, try thinking of it as more than twenty-five per cent instead.

On the other hand, you got what you paid for; the 2.9-litre six-cylinder Healey with 132bhp was spectacularly quicker than the lower order competition, with a top speed of

The Triumph TR4 was the B's other big rival in 1962, but similar performance was offset by a markedly higher price.

about 123mph (198kph) and a sub-10-second 0–60mph (0–96.5kph) time. Unfortunately for the owner, the insurance companies and petrol pumps took that into account too, so the big Healey was a lot more expensive to run, as well as being more expensive to buy.

As for the other options, they were all rather more esoteric. You could have had the glassfibre-bodied V8 engined Daimler SP250, which had been on offer since 1959, with 140bhp and Triumph TR3 based suspension. It was expensive and none too reliable, but it was quick – and had such a problem with chassis flexing that it was not unknown for the doors to pop open.

You could have gone for a Morgan, which wouldn't have been a lot more expensive than a B but would have been a lot more idiosyncratic. You might also have gone for one of Colin Chapman's new Lotus Elans, which gave a lot of performance from their Lotus-developed Ford twin-cam engines, and unsurpassed road-holding; but they were still on the fringe, and they were £1,499 – or a good fifty-eight per cent more than the mass-produced B.

If you weren't totally Anglophile, the Fiat 1500S and Alfa Giulietta both offered brilliant handling, similar performance and masses of character, but only if you wanted to pay at least half as much again as you would for a B.

In the States, you had all those options, plus the domestic Corvette, which was still relatively sporty and cheap, but not Euro-pean and therefore appealing to a subtly different market.

By 1964, there was a different kind of American car, the sporty, youth-orientated Mustang and its siblings, but they were again for the masses, not for the individual who bought a B – and in any case the B had a two-year head start.

And then there was the Datsun 1500 Roadster, which was uncannily like the B for a car which had been launched some time before it. It had the B's slab-sided roundness and it even had recessed headlights, plus mechanical similarities like independent front-suspension with coils and wishbones, live axle rear-suspension on cart springs, and front disc/rear drum braking.

It had Japanese-typical equipment levels and a fair reputation for build quality, but not much yet by way of performance. That came later, first with twin carbs and then with bigger engines, including an 'off-the-shelf' stock racing option. The well equipped Datsun was comfortably cheaper than a fully loaded B, but Japanese cars had a long way to go before they matched the sporting kudos of virtually anything European.

All of that changed over the years, of course, with cars like the Datsun 240Z from Japan and the TR7 from Britain finally overwhelming the ageing B; but that was a long way into the future, when corporate politics and federal legislation also began to erode the B's lead. In the meantime, it had a glorious career to etch out . . .

5 Running modifications – B Roadster

By the end of 1962, over 4,500 MGB Roadsters had left Abingdon, and in the first full year of production, 1963, 23,308 cars were built – just eleven cars short of the best the A ever sold in a single year. It was already clear that the B was a complete commercial success and that the new production regime was going to allow MG to build vastly more cars at the old works than had once been thought possible – a large proportion of them, of course, in left-hand drive form for the massive US market.

Initially, that meant little more than having the steering wheel on the 'wrong' side, with minor differences in things like wiper layout and tail lights, but as the years went by, changing US regulations meant that those cars became increasingly modified – and an ever more uncomfortable thorn in the side of MG's engineers and BL's management.

Without the US market, on the other hand, things would have been very different indeed.

So now, in effect, Abingdon had become more of an assembly plant than a factory – a process which had started to a lesser degree with the A and its shipped-in body and chassis units. That allowed the factory to build not only the A and subsequently the B but also the large and small Healeys (the 100, 3000 and the Sprite), and the Midget – and between 1960 and 1963 there had even been enough spare capacity to build Morris Minor vans and Travellers.

As for the B, the body/chassis units originated from Pressed Steel's new Swindon plant and the floorpan and panel sets were taken by road to the Morris Bodies Branch in Coventry for assembly, painting and partial trimming (and after 1971 the shells were fully assembled at Swindon, then painted and trimmed in Cowley). From there it was back on the road on transporters to Abingdon, there to meet up with all the running gear and road equipment.

All of that, too, came in from various suppliers, both inside and outside of the BMC organisation. And, fortunately, the B was born in a relatively settled period within the often troubled British motor industry, so early production was largely undisturbed by industrial action or parts shortages.

So the B settled quickly into its production run, while the Abingdon engineers kept a constant eye on ways to improve it; and, as was soon to become clear, on ways to expand the range.

CHANGING WITH THE TIMES

The first major modifications to the B came early in 1963 (its first full year of production and when it was still in Roadster-only form), with the offer of optional Laycock D-type overdrive, at £60.8.4d. The overdrive, which effectively increases the overall gearing on selected gears to give more relaxed cruising, operated electrically on third and top gears, controlled from a switch on the dash near the steering column. It became a standard fitting in June 1975, and by 1977 the operating

A very simple, uncluttered look characterised the car as launched, in this case a right-hand drive model with steel wheels and optional front overriders. This is one of the earliest works pre-publicity cars.

switch had been moved from the facia into a more convenient position on the top of the gearchange knob.

In June 1963, the factory offered the attractive glassfibre hard-top as an option for the first time (an option which continued throughout the whole production life of the car, and which was also emulated by several after-market equipment suppliers – though never really as attractively as the works top). The B also gained modified rear springs and a stronger brake lever in 1963, and as early as August 1963 the folding hood replaced the fiddly demountable type as standard kit.

The build-it-yourself type with splitting frame and clip-on covering was fairly awkward to put up or take down in a hurry (particularly while hanging onto your fingernails); the folding type which remained fixed

to the car was considerably easier to handle, but it did take up a good deal of the otherwise useful space behind the seats, where it strapped in place when taken down. In practice, if you wanted to carry anybody or anything in the space at the back you had to have the fixed hood up rather than folded.

In February 1964, closed circuit crankcase breathing (the first rudimentary step towards growing emission controls) was introduced, changing the engine designation from 18G to 18GA; and in October, the oil cooler which had always been offered on export models was made standard, while an electronic rev counter was substituted for the earlier mechanical type.

Most important of all, though, a new five main bearing version of the 1,798cc B-Series engine was introduced, as engine type 18GB.

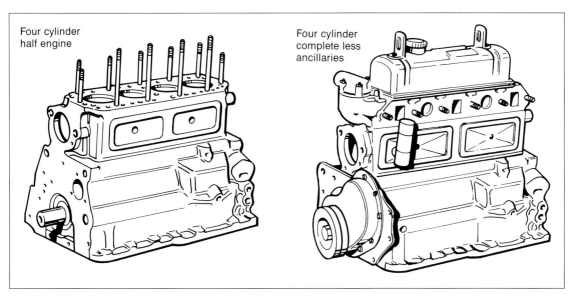

Four cylinder
half engine

Four cylinder
complete less
ancillaries

*The four-cylinder B-Series engine is an uncomplicated basis for
a popular sports car such as the B, with pushrod overhead valve
layout and all porting on the same side of the head.*

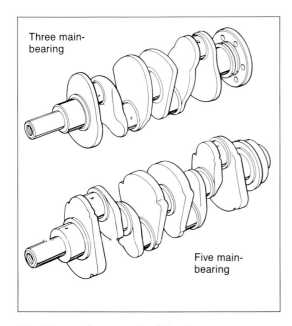

Three main-
bearing

Five main-
bearing

*The biggest change to the B in the
early days was the change in 1964
from a three-bearing to a five-bearing
crankshaft in the B-Series engine, for
better reliability and smoothness.*

The five-bearing engine wasn't designed specifically for the B, but for the newly launched Austin 1800 saloon, which had fortuitously supplied the 1,798cc engine in the first place.

It wasn't so much that the three-bearing bottom end was regarded as being unreliable if properly looked after (although it was prone to occasional high-mileage breakages), more that it was considered too unrefined for the new saloon. Even with a crankshaft damper that had been introduced for the B engine, the three-bearing unit did have a slightly rough period at low revs.

The five bearing unit didn't offer any more power or any more torque according to the factory figures, with both still being listed as before, at 95bhp at 5,400rpm and 110lb ft at 3,000rpm. With a bit more internal friction it didn't rev quite as freely as the three-bearing unit, but it did make the already robust B-Series engine even more unburstable, and it is quite common for this engine to run to 100,000 miles without undue problems.

*If you really can't live with the black grille and Rostyle wheel
look, it's a simple matter to substitute more popular alternatives.
Spotlights and luggage carrier are additions, too.*

ENTER THE B GT

1965 not only saw another round of minor modifications to the Roadster, it also marked the introduction of the B GT, which we will cover separately, and from here on in, modifications to the two models generally ran roughly in parallel – though not always.

New to the Roadster in 1965 were a larger, 12-gallon fuel tank, sealed propshaft bearings, plus a different type of interior door handle and improved locks – a far cry from the days when the A Roadster didn't have locks at all, or even external handles . . .

A front anti-roll bar was standardised from November 1966 – again following the lead of export cars, which had always had the bar as standard, just as they had had the oil cooler as a factory fitment while domestic cars listed it as an option. Such detail differences had a good deal more to do with initial pricing than to do with engineering, of course.

It wasn't entirely coincidental, either, that the roll-bar was standardised only a few months after the launch of the GT, which had it from the start. Very few people had actually complained at the safe, predictable handling of the B with or without the front bar, most simply remarking on its mild understeer, converting progressively to controllable oversteer. The anti-roll bar simply gave slightly more control of that oversteer by limiting the roll angles on the relatively soft springing.

The dash of an early left-hand drive car shows blanked off holes for controls for optional heater and on the far left for overdrive switch. The car has a floor mounted headlamp dip-switch, and map-reading light to the right of the lockable glovebox. Although the look was fairly spartan, it did offer a remarkable amount of room.

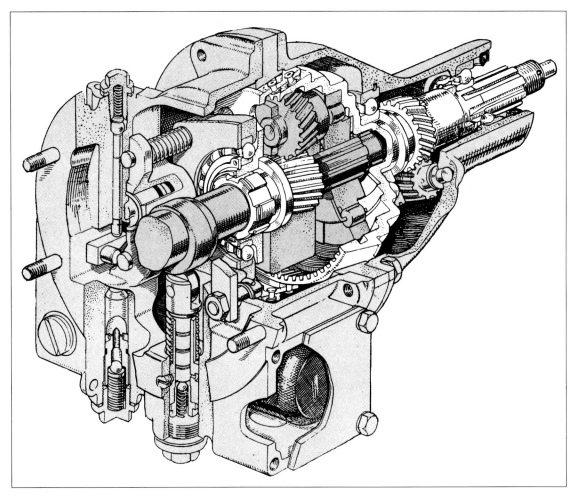

Laycock overdrive was an early and very popular option, giving more relaxed high-speed cruising.

In April 1967, the next signs of a policy of rationalising Roadster and GT running gear appeared, as the Salisbury 'tube-type' rear axle introduced on the GT was adopted for the Roadster too, in place of the earlier, A-type 'banjo'.

It was a substantial improvement, being both stronger and quieter – in fact it had been used on the GT in the first place because the old type was considered simply too noisy on the closed car.

Five years on from the B's launch, in October 1967, when it might have been reasonable to expect that a successor would already have been under development, MG introduced what is generally known as the MkII version of the car – though the official nomenclature is simply 'Fourth Series'. The original car, offically 'Third Series', with the A and the A Twin-Cam being the first two series, retrospectively became known (popularly) as the MkI.

The revised model had an all-synchro gearbox, revised interior with different door trim and seats, alternator rather than dynamo electrics (which implied new, negative-earth polarity), a pre-engaged starter motor, and new reversing lights.

The new gearbox (whose fitting demanded some floorpan changes around the transmission tunnel) survived for the rest of the B's production life, and although it shared internal components with the six-cylinder Austin 3-litre saloon and the new MGC, its outer casing was unique to the B. As well as the easier changes, it offered revised ratios to cheer up those who had always complained of too big a gap between second and third.

Consequently, although the car was slightly heavier by now, the transmission changes (both gearbox and rear axle) had actually made it slightly more accelerative, and the best figures *Motor* magazine ever achieved for a B Roadster were from a car in this spec, in December 1969.

Then, they managed 0–60mph (0–96.5kph) in 11 seconds dead, compared to their previous best of 12.1 (which was with the very first car they tried, back in 1962), and most of the intermediate figures were their best ever, too. Top speed, on the other hand, was marginally down, from 108mph (174kph) to 105mph (169kph).

Synchro on all gears was obviously particularly well received in the States, where being a sports car was good, but being a refined sports car was better; *Road & Track*'s introduction to the new model in July 1968 was headed: 'All-Synchro MGB: Yes, it really is true, the MGB has a fully synchronised gearbox'.

Even more than most people, *Road & Track* were already making quite a thing of the B's 'vintage' character, and there may have been just a touch of wishful thinking in their opening paragraph: 'The MGB has been with us for over five years now and probably has two more years to go. Truly British, its character is now vintage . . .'

There was rather further to go than that.

THE AUTOMATIC OPTION

In the meantime, more radically, the MkII also introduced the option of an automatic gearbox − which might sound like the last thing a traditional sports car needs, and maybe *was* the last thing the B needed.

There was nothing particularly wrong with the unit itself. The Borg-Warner Type 35 three-speed epicyclic gearbox with torque converter was widely used, reliable and effective; and testers were generally kind to its appearance in the B, but maybe a little confused as to why MG had bothered.

Autocar, for instance, in April 1970, commented:

> 'Even nowadays, when open two-seaters are rarely found without wind-down side windows, weather-tight hoods, bodywork that enfolds driver and passenger and some sort of heater, it seems odd that one can buy a medium-size British sports car with automatic transmission. Particularly when the model in question is that most traditionally sporting sports car, the eight-year-old MGB . . . Open two-seat, two-litre automatics are hardly thick on the ground, and we had a hard job deciding on four not-very comparative cars for our data pages.'

The four they did choose were a Ford Capri 2000GT, a Triumph GT6 Mk2, an Opel GT 1900, and a Lotus Elan S4 SE − all manuals and as peculiar a mix as you might wish to find; as they said, they were struggling.

Generally, though, they didn't dislike the automatic option; maximum speeds in the lower holds were 48 (77) and 79mph (127kph) (at 6,000rpm), the normal change-up points were around 38 (61) and 62mph (100kph) (5,000rpm), but *Autocar*'s testers found it better to hold onto the changes until 41 (66) and 67mph (108kph) to compensate for a 'distinct lag in response'. Overall, they found the changes pretty smooth, no difference at all in top speed and only a slight penalty in standing start acceleration, with similar differences in the intermediate times. Surprisingly, fuel consumption was actually *better* than in their last test of a manual car.

As for driving feel, they commented:

'Thanks to the first and second gear holds, one can impress some of one's own ideas on the transmission in the sort of driving an MG is meant for – proper driving, across country, not just in towns. L2 gives one a useful degree of engine braking, selection of second being a little slow but not excessively jerky from the high end of the ratio's range . . . Again, somewhat surprisingly, in spite of the slight slowing of what is not by contemporary international standards a very great performer, the automatic B is remarkably satisfying on the open road.'

Very few B customers ever took the trouble to find out though, because the option lasted only until September 1973, and only around one car in fifty used it. It was never so much as offered as an option on the US market.

MUTED WELCOME FOR THE C

The other radical introduction for 1967, the six-cylinder MGC, was a nice idea in theory – a B with more power and more performance – but it too was a flop with the customers, for reasons which will be discussed later.

With the launch of the MkII, the B also reflected changes in US requirements which were already beginning to stem from the country's new sensitivity to environmental and safety issues, much of which had been brought to national attention by Ralph Nader's crusading book *Unsafe At Any Speed*. And some of what Nader argued was already being enshrined in legislation, starting with President Johnson's 1966 Safety Acts. Implementation of some issues was delayed by legal action on the part of a broad lobby of manufacturers, including MG, but in the long term the new requirements were unavoidable.

Cars bound for the USA gained a totally

Ralph Nader

Ralph Nader has one of the most maligned names in the history of the motor industry. When anyone needs a tag on which to hang the beginning of the modern decline of free-for-all motoring, they automatically evoke Nader's seminal book *Unsafe at Any Speed*, published in 1965, as the apparent catalyst for all the environmental legislation that has followed.

He was born in 1934 and his crusading began when he was a law student at Harvard in the early 1960s, mainly directed at automobile safety. In *Unsafe at Any Speed* he mainly attacked General Motors' (GM) rear-engined Chevy Corvair as being inherently unstable, and Nader, not surprisingly entered into long arguments with GM about the truth of his allegations. Public opinion generally came down on Nader's side as standing up for the small man against the big batallions.

A Senate committee ruled that GM had fulfilled their responsibilities, but sales were ruined, and hundreds of actions were brought. The Corvair was dropped in 1969.

Nader then sued GM for harassment after they had him followed and investigated by private detectives, and he won.

He used the substantial damages to set up a consumer watchdog organisation, and expanded his crusading interests to all things consumer and environmental, making both friends and enemies along the way.

The motor industry always remained a target, not just from US manufacturers; he also attacked Jaguar in the late 1970s and was particularly scathing of the VW Beetle.

He is widely seen as the catalyst for most of the American legislation which so badly affected the B (and everything else), beginning with the National Traffic and Motor Vehicle Safety Act in 1966, and he has never stopped campaigning since.

Yet, although Nader and all he has stood for has been derided as a thorn in the side of the industry, he has probably done an immense amount of long-term good. He *has* promoted safety (albeit in a flamboyant way which many resent as self-publicising), and he has promoted a cleaner environment – a small price to pay for all that.

Immaculate engine in a late 1960's B Roadster shows the impressive accessibility which makes the B such an attractive proposition for enthusiastic home mechanics.

redesigned, heavily padded dash (with no glovebox), an energy absorbing steering column and dual-circuit brakes from October 1967.

More fundamentally, the B for the US market sprouted emission control equipment for the first time, with modified carbs and manifolding – and that marked the beginning of a steady decline in power for US engines which eventually resulted in 'Federalised' Bs, running on a single Zenith-Stromberg carb, giving an asthmatic 65bhp in their most strangled form.

With all the extra weight they were obliged to cart around too, late US Bs could barely get out of their own way, and it's probably a miracle that sales held up even for as long as they did . . .

A BREAK WITH TRADITION

1968 was the first year since its launch in which the B went through a whole season without a listed change, but there was enough to make up for that in 1969 with the controversial switch from the pretty and traditionalist-satisfying chrome grille of the original to a rather blander black recessed design. The change coincided with MG's absorption into the Austin Morris Division of British Leyland and was foisted upon Abingdon by Longbridge – where it was styled, with little apparent sympathy for the still powerful MG spirit. The new corporate identity was rubbed home with small BL badges on the front wings.

Rostyle wheels replaced the earlier pressed steel discs (with the ever popular wires remaining on the options list), and there were new rubber inserts in the bumper over-riders. Inside, there were minor changes to the facia, updated, vinyl-covered reclining seats with optional headrests, a rather nice leather rimmed three-spoked steering wheel, and a dipping rear view mirror. US cars had

minor changes to their tail lamps, and side repeater lamps replaced the simple reflectors that had been on their cars since 1969's models. For the 1970 model year only, US cars had a split rear bumper with a different number plate style.

With its black recessed grille and vinyl seats, though, it would be fair to say that this was not one of the more popular models, even though the changes were only superficial.

STILL A BIG SELLER

Any fears, though, that the B would have been dead and buried by the 1970s were being given the lie by ever increasing sales, and 1970 was the best year so far, with over 36,000 cars built (around sixty-five per cent of them Roadsters).

The changes for that year were largely inside the car, with an improved ventilation system, a steering lock and a new interior courtesy light, but there were minor body changes too with self-locking boot and bonnet stays in place of the old props, and a better folding hood, styled by Michelotti.

It was another heavy year for US modifications though, with emissions control being taken another step further with a power-sapping engine-driven air pump, and inertia-reel seat belts being standardised. Although US engines still had their twin SU carburettors at this stage, the Federal emission control mods and a low 8.0:1 compression ratio had already knocked power down to a rather miserable 82bhp at 5,400rpm. Cars for the even more sensitive Californian market even had to use catalyst systems from 1974 on, and that meant using unleaded fuel and suitably low compression ratios. It was hardly surprising that the B was no longer a 100mph (160kph) car in US trim.

In October 1971, when the B entered its Fifth Series, or MkIII, it underwent further changes inside aimed largely at giving the car a more comfortable image. It now

The new look from 1969 included Rostyle pressed wheels and unpopular recessed black grille without traditional surround – foisted on MG by British Leyland. This is a 1971 US spec car, with rubber overrider inserts.

sprouted neat rocker switches in its new centre console, and a centre armrest cum oddment bin, while the GT gained nylon seat inserts. The radio (or more accurately, the space for the radio, which was still an option) was moved from the centre of the dash to where the speaker used to be, in the console behind the gearlever. That left a convenient space in the centre of the dash for some very welcome, swivelling fresh air vents. And the US padded facia simultaneously found a way of accommodating a glovebox.

There were other practical improvements too, with the collapsible steering column first seen on US market cars being offered on all cars. And there was an improved engine for some markets – the final significant engine change, which would see the car through to the end of its run. The best of the revised engines was the bigger-valved 18V type, but later 18V engines reverted to smaller valves.

WHAT THE PEOPLE WANT . . .

The unpopular recessed black grille was unceremoniously dropped in 1972 after surviv-

BL soon felt the error of their ways with the black grille models and reverted to something more traditional during 1972, on the 'MkIII', with many detail changes inside.

ing for just a couple of years. It was replaced by a new black mesh centre but with the old chrome rim and vertical centre bar reinstated – much to the delight of all those who still saw the echoes of Kimber's original design in the modern idiom.

The GT gained full nylon seats and a seat-belt warning light was added – the seat-belt type having recently been changed to the fixed lock 'one-handed' type. Inertia reel belts were a new option, and the tonneau cover was at last made standard on the UK market. There was another slight change of steering wheel design, the round holes of the old style giving way to slots. Padded arm-rests on the doors gave a slightly more up-market look, and there was a new cigarette

lighter on the standard equipment list; engines weren't allowed to smoke any more but passengers still were . . .

Radial ply tyres were standardised for the British market, too, late in 1972 – and by September 1973 they were standard for all markets, giving the B a slightly softer ride and improved road-holding.

. . . AND WHAT THE PEOPLE GET

Nothing more exciting than new badges raised their heads in 1973, and the automatic gearbox option finally fizzled out with very few people caring one way or the other; but it

A steering wheel with round holes also came with the 1969 changes, and this car has non-standard gauges in the centre console.

was just a lull before the storm, and in 1974 the B changed forever, and the real downhill slide probably began.

The problem was US legislation. The solution was the infamous 'rubber bumpers' and all that went with them.

MG already knew that they had to meet the new regulations, and late in 1973 they fitted some US cars with an interim solution comprising enormous (and enormously ugly) rubber overriders.

The infamous 5mph (8kph) bumpers followed late in 1974. They had a heavy steel core and a 'fared-in' outer covering which was reaction moulded in Bayer's new material Bayflex, by Marleyfoam Ltd; and, ugly as they were, had that been as far as the modifications had gone, they might not have been so badly received.

The real problem was that alongside the bumpers (which added around five inches (12.5cm) to the length of the car), the B had to suffer a 1½in (3.8cm) increase in ride height to bring the bumpers up to the standard height dictated by US regulations. The new bumpers were heavier (especially at the front), which was a penalty that the increasingly strangled Bs for the US market did not need, but that was not the most damaging spin-off; that was to be to the handling.

The increased ride height, coupled with the B's relatively soft springing, which was unchanged, imposed substantially more body roll, which in turn meant a marked increase in roll oversteer – enough, in fact, to reduce overall road-holding.

Because the B was essentially a very forgiving car in its transition to oversteer,

The GT had an extended range from 1965, and generally followed the styling themes of the Roadster, including grilles.

and with excellent steering feel, the changed characteristics certainly weren't dangerous, but they did make the rear end more twitchy, and magazines at the time seemed to delight in showing pictures of rubber-bumpered Bs with ridiculous roll angles being hurled through test track corners on large armfulls of opposite lock.

Unfortunately, even though European legislation didn't yet demand the US-style changes, Europe was stuck with them too, mainly, of course, because MG simply couldn't afford to build two distinct versions of all the B variants.

For the same reason, although the B GT was sadly withdrawn from the US market (in favour of the TR7), it was still modified in the same way – with both bumper and ride-height changes.

There was another reason for the GT's demise in the States: emission requirements were based on car weight and the GT was just

heavy enough to make it need even more de-toxing work than the Roadster. MG could see little point in spending an enormous amount of money that they frankly didn't have to legalise a car that would then probably have had the performance of a push-bike.

And sadly for owners of rubber-bumper cars, the sheet metal changes made to the car to accommodate them are such that it is horribly difficult to change back to chrome bumpers. Not impossible, but certainly difficult.

Buried among the howls of protest at the new look, a switch from the old twin 6-volt battery system to a simpler 12-volt battery attracted little attention, although standardised hazard warning lights were obviously intended to. The overdrive was changed from the Laycock D-type to the improved Laycock LH, and the ratio was changed marginally.

In June 1975, overdrive finally became a standard fitment rather than an option. The

The biggest change of all came on 1975 models, with the 'rubber bumpers' forced on MG by US safety requirements. The car also needed increased ride height, which unbalanced both looks and handling.

single Zenith-Stromberg carburettor had been foisted on MG by US requirements late in 1974, and maybe in sheer embarrassment the MGB badge was dropped from the bootlid of US cars.

SIGNS OF DESPERATION

In what was officially celebrated as MG's 50th anniversary year, 1975, it was clear that drastic steps were more necessary than ever if the B was to survive, let alone thrive.

The anniversary was marked with a 'Jubilee' edition of the B GT (but not the Roadster). The cars were mechanically standard, but smartened up in finest marketing opportunist tradition with a new coat of paint (in this case British Racing Green with gold stripes), some additional badges and one or

two other bits of low-budget glitz. There was a tinted windscreen for instance, V8-style alloy wheels with bigger tyres, overdrive, and head restraints on the seats.

They were nice enough looking cars, admittedly, but the buying public, unfortunately, could hardly contain their indifference.

As for the mainstream models, with the B now beginning to mark time to its ultimate demise, 1975 was another 'no-change' year, and 1976's changes really showed that BL were trying desperately to breathe some life into falling B sales without being able (or willing) to make fundamental changes.

From 1972's record sales of over 39,000 examples of all variants of the B (GT and Roadster), sales had dived by almost 10,000 in 1973, slipped a little further in 1974 and hit a worrying low of only just over 24,500 in 1975. That means that in three years sales had slumped by a disastrous thirty-seven and a half per cent. They pulled back a little in 1976, to just over 29,500 – but from there it was downhill all the way to the end in 1980.

As we shall see later when we look at the decline of the B and at what might have followed, the problem was not that Abingdon was devoid of ideas for a B replacement; far from it. The Farina styled EX234 project which could have replaced both the B and the Midget was already on the stocks by 1967, and the spectacular mid-engined AD021 had reached mock-up form by late 1970.

What's more, the MGB GT V8 which was launched in August 1973, as the second attempt at putting a bigger engined B on the market, really could have been a very good car indeed. In the end, it stayed as a GT model only, it never went to the USA, and it was never built in anything like the numbers it deserved to be – which BL always blamed on supply problems, but which, as we will see later, really had a great deal to do with the political relationship between MG and Triumph.

Certainly, then, Abingdon, *could* have

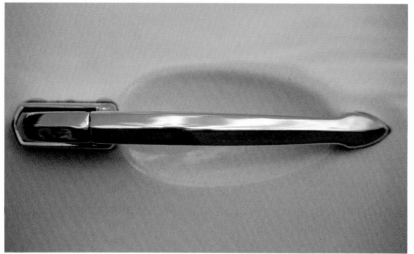

The Rostyle wheels actually suit the elegant lines of the GT rather better than they do the Roadster.

replaced the B; they simply weren't allowed to. Thanks to internal politics and increasingly desperate financial straits within the parent organisation, MG's talented team simply wasted their time on token and cosmetic updates, until, in the end, MG itself all but died and the talk turned not to replacements but to rescue.

The B still had a few years' grace before that happened, of course, but attitudes towards it were changing subtly – to a quite open stance that the B's time had surely come.

FRUSTRATED AFFECTION

Autocar's test of a rubber-bumpered Roadster in April 1975 was typical, and they nailed their colours to the mast right from their introduction:

'The MGB, Britain's most successful sports car, has now been with us for nearly 13 years. Of late, there have been only detail changes, the most obvious of which is the very cleverly blended "soft-front" 5mph bumpers, reaction-moulded by Messrs Marleyfoam Ltd out of Bayflex 90 polyurethane, and the 1½in increase in ride height, adopted to meet American bumper height dictates. There are other smaller changes, though few notable which might have removed some of the B's long-criticized defects. At the announcement of British Leyland's new contender for the American market, the TR7, we gathered that the MGB's existence was not threatened – a good thing, since the MG name still carries more successful and deep-seated sporting associations than the less laurel-winning one of Triumph, which is one reason for continuing it – and that it was, in the words of a British Leyland executive, expected "to soldier on as it is" – not such a good thing . . .'

Ironically, *Autocar*, like virtually every other magazine that began its tests in such terms, still really quite liked the car. They reported 'tolerable' performance, commented on handling that had deteriorated with the roll-oversteer induced by the new ride-height but which was still essentially entertaining and forgiving, and they thought the car was more comfortable than ever.

When it came to their summing up, though, the frustration was clear:

'It is obvious that the MGB more than ever needs some redesign. We feel that it would be bad sales policy for British Leyland either to drop the MGB in any of its markets since the MG name is still better known to the enthusiast, or simply let the car continue unimproved, since it is already far behind some of its international competitors. A new B is needed now, more than ever before, an open car of modern design, especially in suspension and performance, and preferably with a better convertible arrangement than the old-fashioned fabric hood. At the same time, one does not envy the body designer who has to follow such a pleasant-looking sports car, which is still, in spite of its failings, many of the things that a sports car should be.'

FALLING ON DEAF EARS

Ah, if only BL could have recognised the well-meaning mix of affection and frustration in pieces like that, which were being repeated *ad infinitum* in magazines on both sides of the Atlantic by this time. Blinded, though, by their insistence on pushing the TR7 (a mistake alluded to in *Autocar*'s introduction above), BL continued to let the B wallow on – now almost literally.

In the middle of 1976, the Roadster got a zip-in rear window, a new facia, and deckchair striped seat material – plus halogen headlamps on UK models, which at least gave the driver a chance to see where the car was no longer going.

After listening to fourteen years of criticism they finally changed the pedal layout slightly, to allow heel and toe braking and gearchanging for the first time. They moved the overdrive switch into the top of the lever, and they added a stiffer front roll bar, plus a standard anti-roll bar at the rear, to moderate the effects of the new, taller suspension. At the same time the steering ratio was reduced, to give three and a half turns between locks instead of three, in what seemed like a move in the opposite direction.

It wasn't nearly so big a move in the opposite direction, though, as dropping the V8 rather than having a real go at making it work commercially as well as it did technically.

The revised interior from late 1976 was very neat but also fell into BL's 'deckchair' interior design period, which now looks horribly dated.

THE FINAL DAYS

And that, so far as anything of any consequence at all, was that. Inertia reel belts were standardised in 1977, door-mounted radio speakers and an aerial were standardised early in 1978, and rear foglamps were fitted as standard on UK cars in June 1980 – by which time the B had only four months left to run.

Perhaps the final indignity was that 1980 US market cars, to comply with legislation in the land of the blanket 55mph (88kph) speed limit, were fitted with 80mph (128kph) speedometers . . .

As already recounted, the news that MG production at Abingdon was to end came, with extraordinary insensitivity, on 10 September 1979 – on the Monday after week-long celebrations of fifty years of production at the famous plant.

Far from laying down and accepting their fate, MG people from around the world rallied to try to save the cause, as we shall

see later, and there were several attempts to save the B itself – some more serious than others.

It didn't happen, though; irrevocable confirmation that the B was not to be rescued after all came in July 1980, and the car now just ran its natural course until the final examples emerged.

Pressed Steel had their own small ceremony after they had built the final GT body on 1 October and the final Roadster on 2 October. According to their figures they had made 387,184 B Roadster shells and 125,618 B GT shells, for a total of 512,802 Bs. On top of that they listed 4,542 C Roadsters and 4,457 C GTs for a total of 8,999, and 2,591 V8 GTs. That gave totals of 391,726 open cars and 132,666 GTs – or a grand overall score of 524,392 shells in eighteen years.

Thinking back to John Thornley's agreement to pay an additional £2 per shell in lieu of the larger initial contract, Pressed Steel probably thought they had done fairly well out of the B in the end . . .

Not quite every shell that left Pressed Steel's Stratton St Margaret works ended up as a complete car of course, but BL's official figures for the final total of all models was 521,111 cars – a staggering number for a company whose previous single-model record was just 101,081, from all variants of the A.

HALF A MILLION Bs

The last two Bs, a Roadster and a GT, came off the Abingdon lines on 22 and 23 October 1980. In the meantime, Syd Enever, Don Hayter, Terry Mitchell and John O'Neill had managed what must have been a rather ironic smile for the cameras as the 500,000th B, a left-hand drive Roadster, came off the line in January 1980.

And alongside the final run of standard cars, MG built another specially-liveried car, the Limited Edition (LE).

They built 1,000 examples of this LE, the 420 Roadsters in metallic bronze and the 580 GTs in metallic pewter, both with the inevitable commemorative side stripes (gold on Roadsters, silver on GTs), plus a choice of wire or special alloy wheels.

It was a fine final piece of opportunism. The kit had first appeared late in 1979 on an 'Exclusive New "Limited Edition" MGB' for the States, listed as a 1980 model. Launched at the New York Show in late summer, this US-only version came in any colour you liked so long as it was black, with a silver stripe incorporating a Union Jack with MGB lettering.

It also had the same five-spoke alloy wheels from GKN which the final LE version would offer, with wider profile, 185/70 radial tyres,

and a smaller, chunkier leather steering wheel. There was a front air-dam to distinguish it from ordinary models, too, plus a stainless steel luggage rack and additional foot mats. Everything came as standard except the rack and mats.

According to the MG News section of *MG Magazine*, 5,000 copies of the US Limited Edition were to be built 'or about 25 per cent of annual B exports to the US'. At $8,550 suggested retail price at East and West coast ports of entry, it was $600 more than the standard 1980 convertible. Surprisingly, perhaps, they also reported that MG sales figures in the USA for July 1979 had achieved a new record, at 4,068 units for the month – comfortably beating 1977's record of 3,774.

The standard cars' British price in these final months had reached £6,127 for the Roadster and £6,595 for the GT, with UK versions of the Limited Edition models at £6,445 and £6,937 respectively.

In practice, the LE models, although already built of course, didn't go on sale until early in 1981, and when they did so they sold very slowly indeed.

The very last cars off the line were a Roadster and a GT, both in LE livery and both of which went into BL's Heritage Museum.

The last US-spec B had gone to Henry Ford II and thence to the Henry Ford Museum in Dearborn, where it would sit alongside a 1930 M-Type Midget which Henry I had bought way back then. The last export car, a Roadster, went to Japan.

There was no longer any chance of a reprieve for the B, or – for the time being at least – for MG, but the official end of production was far from being the end of the B story . . .

6 The B GT

Two of the most quoted views of John Thornley are his expressed ambition to build 'a poor man's Aston Martin', and, once he had achieved it (but before the car was shown to the public), his declaration: 'We've produced a motor car now in which no managing director would be ashamed to turn up at the office.'

Thornley (and Syd Enever) never made any secret of the fact that what they really wanted most of all was to build a GT version of the B, but they were also realists enough to accept that the public wanted the open top car first and so that was the way it was done. It was only a matter of time before they had their way, though, and in October 1965, three years after the B Roadster had taken its bow in the same hall, they saw their dream launched to the public at the London Motor Show in Earls Court.

A NEW SHAPE

As with the launch of the Roadster, there was a split-down-the-middle exhibition model on display; round the bottom of its plinth were the very apposite words: 'MG Magic In A New Shape.'

And, by general consensus, a very attractive new shape it was, too. It was called, simply and accurately enough, the MGB GT.

Officially, it began as project EX227 – and it only started taking shape during 1964, after the launch of the B Roadster. In reality, it had been on the cards for a lot longer than that, as Thornley's opening quote reveals.

To see just *how* important a GT car was to the Abingdon team at the time, you can certainly look back as far as the A, even for

starters. By 1956, just a year after its introduction, the A could be equipped with a stylish glassfibre factory hardtop, with sliding side screens – which gave the basic roadster a few of the creature comforts which the management obviously already thought desirable. It attached to the unstressed body using the normal hood frame pivot points for brackets and looked quite attractive – if a little 'tacked-on'. The lower body didn't need to change for the hardtop, of course, which meant that the A still had its usual internal door handles and non-existent security arrangements. The hardtop, not too surprisingly, became quite popular among A rally drivers.

In October 1956, the idea was taken a logical stage further, when a genuine coupe version of the A was launched at the Earls Court Motor Show.

It was an exceptionally handsome conversion and it went a good way further than just putting a fixed roof over the passengers' heads. The flat windscreen of the roadster was replaced by a wrap around screen which blended neatly round to slim front roof pillars, which even had quarter-lights fixed to them. The rear window was also a full wrap around type, albeit with the glass split by two vertical ribs. These were meant as much for strengthening as for styling, as the top did tend to flex slightly. Using the ribs meant that the designers could keep the rear three-quarter pillars down to reasonable dimensions, too, making visibility perfectly acceptable.

And MG had really gone the whole hog on creature comforts this time, giving the A coupe both wind-up windows (with fixed door frames) and even external door handles. The handles' neat but awkward shape showed just what a problem trying to blend them into the A's extraordinarily smooth lines had presented on the roadster.

In every respect, though, the A coupe was a successful exercise. It was aesthetically handsome, aerodynamically a little better than the roadster (enough to give it a higher top speed, even though it was obviously heavier), roomy, light and airy inside, and it turned the A into a genuinely different kind of car. It was enough of a commercial success, too, to run alongside the various versions of the roadster right through the A's production life, to July 1962. That means it appeared as the MGA 1500 Coupe, the MGA 1600 Coupe, the MGA 1600 MkII and even the MGA Twin Cam Coupe. Whatever else it proved, it proved to Abingdon that there was a demand for a hardtop version of their sports cars and that remained an important consideration when the B was being conceived.

THINKING TOWARDS THE B GT

There were two other kinds of A coupe: racers and styling exercises, both of which clearly showed that the GT theme was never far below the surface of Abingdon thinking.

The works ran production-shape A coupes in many racing and rallying events, but they also ran one car for a private entrant which had much more to do with the B's simultaneous development. This one-off racing A coupe appeared at Le Mans in 1960 and it was a quite different shape from the production car – a fastback rather than just a roadster with a bubble dropped on top.

It was a Don Hayter design, and there's no doubt that it bore a passing resemblance at the rear to the Aston Martins that he had worked on before he arrived at Abingdon. Around the windscreen and door pillars and as far back as the rear edge of the wind-up side windows, it was pure production coupe,

MG never had any doubt that there would eventually be a GT version of the B; as early as 1956, the coupe version of the A showed that they were well aware of the market.

but the roofline then swept on back to what would have been the lower boot edge, with triangular side windows let into the flanks. Where the bootlid would have been there was a huge, quick-release fuel filler.

Running with a highly developed 1,762cc, Weber carburetted version of the Twin-Cam engine, and driven by northern MG racing stalwart Ted Lund (with co-driver Colin Escott) it won the 2-litre prototype class in the 1960 24 Hours, and took 12th place overall, averaging a little over 91mph (146kph). The car ran with the road registration SRX 210 and having finished the race, Lund drove it back to England!

There was no mistaking the resemblance of the Lund car, either, to Hayter's fastback coupe in the series of styling exercises which eventually led to the B.

That was EX205/1, the car which had gradually evolved into the first full-sized model for what was planned as the A's replacement. The full-size exercise was the styling model with the 'registration' BMC 1959, as described earlier, which was completed in 1958, well ahead of the racing fastback – and also, of course, ahead of the final B Roadster shape.

Unlike the B GT, it would have used a conventional boot opening below the rear window, rather than a hatchback – even though the Astons which Hayter had worked on already had the pioneering feature of a fully opening tailgate; perhaps that would have been just too close to the Aston design for comfort at the time. It was also rather larger than the B eventually turned out to be – of which more later.

In 1961 the Lund car ran at Le Mans again, in a further developed form; its nose was redesigned with a much rounder look, throwing away the grille and leaving just a narrow slot for the radiator air intake, and additional vents for brake cooling ducts. The wings were also reshaped, recessing the headlamps very slightly in a way which clearly followed the early B styling models.

Although it was now capable of close on 140mph (225kph) it retired within the first hour with engine problems.

There should also have been a works A project at Le Mans for 1961, but the usual problems of corporate management's resistance to racing meant that it never appeared.

Aston Martin lines were also apparent in the fastback styling variant on the Frua EX214 prototype, although that, too, never progressed beyond the model stage; and around the time when the 205/1 and 205/2 exercises (the aforementioned GT and a roadster) were being worked on, Syd Enever commented: 'We've got to back it both ways until things find their own level. We should find out whether the GT style sells better – we should like it that way . . .'

ROADSTER FIRST, AND THE BERLINETTE

Much as they would have liked to concentrate on their GTs, though, Thornley and Enever had to accept that, for the usual commercial reasons, the B Roadster *would* be launched first – and then they had to see one other thoroughly professional attempt at producing a fastback coupe version of the B before their own appeared.

That was the Berlinette MGB 1800, styled and built by Jacques Coune of Brussels and shown for the first time at the Brussels Motor Show in January 1964 – a clear twenty months before the real thing appeared in London in 1965. It was obviously regarded as very handsome, *Car* magazine in March 1965 remarked, with the sort of sexism that they'd never get away with nowadays, 'At £480 extra, it's the tart-trap of the year . . .'

Coune specialised in modifying production cars, and also ran a successful garage and repair business in Brussels – which included agencies for Abarth cars and exhaust systems, for the potent US V8-engined Iso Rivolta, and for Bertone.

With the B GT, Pininfarina achieved what MG themselves for once couldn't, blending top and bottom halves to make a car of enduring elegance.

The Jacques Coune Berlinetta beat MG's own GT to the gun,
but was an expensive alternative once the works car arrived.

Coune didn't approach the problem with half measures. Unlike the soon-to-appear B GT, his car was significantly different below the waistline as well as above.

The windscreen was removed first, then the rear flanks chopped away to leave only the rear wheelarches and the floorpan behind the rear door edges. The front wings were cut well back and the headlamps were set behind Jaguar E-Type-like plexiglass fairings; the rear was then rebuilt, and extended to give a near vertical Kamm tail, with simple round rearlight clusters. There was an external hatch over the enlarged, fully carpeted boot and there was also access to the luggage space from inside the car, which had gained proper, folding, rear seats.

All the minor changes to the Coune Berlinette's bodywork (the roof, the rear flanks and the tail) were in glassfibre, although the new windscreen pillars were in steel, for strength. A new box-section cross-member, welded into place across the car between the rear wheelarches, reinstated the stiffness taken away with the chopping of the rear metal bodywork of the original – and there was considerably more sheet metal strengthening welded into the tail area and bonded into the glassfibre sections. A fair amount of sound deadening material was sandwiched between the new skins at the rear, too, which underlined Coune's up-market intentions.

Most of his small workforce of body builders were Italians whom he had imported from Turin or Milan and thanks to their skills the Berlinette's build quality was extremely impressive for a low volume car.

As on the B GT that was soon to follow, the windscreen became an integral part of the

First public glimpse of the B GT, in 1965, showed just how well the car had worked, retaining all the character of the Roadster with the added practicality of the hardtop.

top on Coune's car, and the whole car was *almost* nice – but looking at it now it has dated a great deal more than the classic shape that MG themselves ultimately adopted.

A LITTLE HELP FROM THE WORKS

Although there is no evidence that this project was anything but a pure freelance restyling exercise, it is true that the first Coune Berlinette was built on a chassis supplied with MG's help by someone with strong company connections. He was Walter Oldfield, who was manager of the Nuffield Press, the vast printing arm of Nuffield's former empire, and he was looking for the fun of a B but with a level of comfort slightly more in step with his mature years. Mr Oldfield apparently met Jacques Coune at the 1963 London Motor Show, and commissioned the car soon afterwards.

The 'donor' car was shipped to Brussels in 1963, as a more or less bare, but mechanically complete, B Roadster; the Coune Berlinette which it was turned into was delivered early in 1964, soon after the model's Brussels Show launch.

Whether or not they deliberately supplied the basic shell to test Coune's concept, MG's designers, particularly Enever, obviously took an interest in Oldfield's car once it showed up in Oxford. It underwent a fairly detailed appraisal at Abingdon, but so far as MG and BMC were concerned, that was as far as their direct interest went.

Coune went on to build fifty-eight examples of his car, which cost around £480 over and above the standard Roadster on which it was based. MG, of course, went their own way and when the official B GT went into full-scale production it turned the Berlinette into an interesting, and now very valuable, but ultimately doomed, red-herring. Even if you'd preferred the Berlinette's attractive looks and revised interior, by October 1965 you would have had a works option for some twenty-five per cent less outlay.

Before the real thing appeared, there was also one other 'in-house' scheme for a B GT, in this case a racing fastback with a very streamlined roofline, based mechanically on the Roadster. The idea came from BMC Competitions Department boss Stuart Turner, and was aimed at the 1965 Le Mans race, but it didn't progress beyond a first discussions stage.

THE PININFARINA TOUCH

While all this was happening, Abingdon were struggling to some extent to make their own ideas work. Another of Thornley's classic sayings at the time was: 'Couldn't we put a shed on it?' – and that was how he often

The rear door solution was admirably neat.

The Luggage Space.

described his GT concept, as just a Roadster with a shed on it . . .

The Abingdon designers' problem was that they just couldn't make the 'shed' look right on top of the curvaceous B body: the bottom was obviously right, the top was apparently right, but the two simply didn't work together.

In the end, they sent the whole project over to Pininfarina, in Turin, to see what they could do with it – and in very short order back came the definitive MGB GT shape.

What Pininfarina had mainly achieved was to marry the angular top, which was so typical of their contemporary work, to the sleekly rounded Roadster bottom, with no uncomfortable visual join. But more than that, Pininfarina had spotted and changed the one thing that had been spoiling all of Abingdon's efforts, the height of the roofline.

Where Abingdon had worked around the standard Roadster windscreen height and line, Pininfarina made the screen deeper and changed its rake, at the same time blending it directly into the bodywork without the separate alloy frame. The side window layout was changed accordingly, the rear tailgate became a full hatchback, and there was the B GT in all its timeless elegance.

Abingdon and Longbridge were obviously delighted, but had they looked back a couple of years, they might have seen a clear clue to

The special-bodied Healey 3000 from the 1962 Geneva Show, built by Pininfarina to competition-winning design, gives clear clues to the eventual B GT roofline.

Pininfarina

Societa Anonima Carrozzeria Pinin Farina was formed in Turin in 1930. Its founder, Battista (Pinin) Farina was already well established as a master coachbuilder, working from his brother's factory. Pinin's own studio and works were set up with considerable support from Vincenzo Lancia, among others, and a great deal of his early work was for Lancia. The company was highly respected from its beginnings, and other companies using Farina's services in the early days included Alfa–Romeo, Hispano–Suiza and Fiat – especially for sporting cars.

After World War II, Pinin Farina continued to work for Lancia and Alfa (notably with the beautiful Aurelia Spider in 1954, and then with the Giulietta Spider) and had broadened his scope with cars like the Cisitalia coupe. What's more, the house became very closely involved with Ferrari from that marque's inception in 1947, and has styled the vast majority of Ferraris ever since. On the mass production side, he began a long association with Peugeot in the 1950s, and in the late 1950s moved to a larger, modern factory at Grugliasco, near Turin.

Pinin took a back seat in 1959, handing day to day running over to his son Sergio, and the same year saw the beginning of the styling house's special relationship with BMC.

The first car to come from that was the angular Austin A40 saloon, followed by numerous other models with the distinctive 'Pininfarina' look.

The change of name from Pinin Farina to Pininfarina was bestowed by the Italian government, which decreed that the company was now so well known that the names were inseparable.

Pinin himself died in 1966 and Sergio took over as president, vastly expanding the company's research and development side into one of the most modern facilities in the world, at the same time adding substantially increased production capacity for the body manufacturing part of the operation.

The new technical facilities at Grugliasco were one of the reasons why the MGB GT could be readied so quickly for production in Britain – because Pininfarina's modern computer systems were able to provide working drawings virtually as soon as the designs had been approved. The other reason that the GT happened so quickly, of course, was simply Pininfarina's remarkable flair.

Today, Pininfarina is still one of the world's greatest styling houses, with very, very few designs which have been less than magnificent. With cars like the Ferrari Dino, the Testarossa, the Alfa Romeo 164 and the F40 in the Pininfarina portfolio, the B GT was a small but significant part of a very illustrious line.

---

the final roofline. It appeared on a special Pininfarina-bodied version of the Austin–Healey 3000, at the 1962 Geneva Show – even before the B Roadster had taken the stage. The car was built by Pininfarina but it was styled by three young students from Ulm University in a styling competition for the prestigious motoring annual *Automobile Year*, part of the prize being to have the car built at Grugliasco.

The car appeared again later in the year at the London Motor Show – the same London Motor Show where the B Roadster was launched. *Motor Sport* magazine couldn't have known how close to the truth they were when they commented of the prizewinning coupe: 'At the moment there are no plans to put the car on the market, but with BMC one never knows.'

The one thing they maybe *didn't* think about was the roofline's in-house migration from the big Healey to the relatively modest B, but then they would have reckoned without Thornley's admirable 'poor man's Aston' philosophy. Thornley also knew that customer expectations were becoming more sophisticated too, explaining at the time of the GT's launch: 'The average age of our

customers has gone up and up, partly forced up by the insurance companies' strictness on the young, partly by the better acceptance of the modern sports car with its more sophisticated design and gentler suspension, instead of the kidney-shaking type of thing we had years ago . . .'

For once, BMC apparently agreed – and didn't prevaricate. Virtually as soon as the GT was seen it was approved, Pininfarina's design drawings went to Pressed Steel and tooling began for a launch as quickly as it could be arranged.

A PRICE TO BE PAID

Although the GT did, therefore, go into production with remarkable speed, there was some element of compromise on Thornley and Enever's side. They would have liked to have taken advantage of the fully stressed top to allow them to pare some of the still rather excessive weight from the bottom.

That, remember, is the one unavoidable penalty of slicing the top off a unitary construction shell: like an eggshell, it is immensely strong when it is complete, but loses out considerably once it has been opened. For the Roadster, the rigidity inevitably lost via the big hole in the top was compensated for by very hefty engineering of what was left below the waistline. Given a proper free hand with the closed and therefore inherently much more rigid GT, a lot of that lower deck reinforcement (and therefore a lot of weight) could have been cheerfully dispensed with.

Taking that to an even more extreme con-

Under the bonnet, and largely under the skin, the B GT was
mechanically identical to the Roadster.

clusion, MG could have kept to roughly the same weight (and therefore roughly the same power to weight ratio without changing engines) but built a slightly bigger car – just as they had actually intended to back in the days of the original EX205/1 model.

And if they had done that, *plus* offering some of the V4 and V6 engine options under consideration at the time, they would have beaten Ford to the gun by a good five years with what turned out to be the Capri philosophy.

In introducing the MkI Capri in 1969, Ford launched what they saw as a 'European' car, in a fastback, sporting saloon shape with a choice of engines which grew steadily over the years. Ford called the Capri 'the car you've always promised yourself' and it captured more customers from other makes than any other Ford model. With the MkII, introduced in 1974, Ford even offered a lifting tailgate, B GT style – plus a lot more room inside and the option of a lot more performance. It would give the B GT a very hard time in the sales war . . .

As it was, although Abingdon had the ideas, there was neither the time nor the money to do anything remotely that ambitious between Roadster and GT, although there was rather more to the new car than was apparent from an outside glance.

Most of the changes were at floorpan level and mostly around the rear of the car. As well as re-engineering the area between the rear wheelarches to incorporate a proper, if occasional, rear seat and some very useful luggage space, MG also took the opportunity to make the one major mechanical modification between Roadster and GT. That was the adoption of the quieter, more robust Salisbury type rear axle, which also found its way onto the Roadster in 1967 as the range was rationalised.

As well as the new rear axle, the GT also gained stiffer springs at the rear to match the extra weight – but not stiff enough to spoil the supple ride, which was such a feature of the B's nature. The springs were the same as had been fitted to 'Police-spec' B Roadsters, to cope with the extra weight of equipment that those cars carried, and the GT also had slightly wider wheels than the Roadster as standard, again to accommodate the extra weight.

The front anti-roll bar (which was still only an option on the Roadster) came as standard on the GT, along with slightly stiffer springs at that end, too, thus preserving the B's safe, balanced handling characteristics in the face of a small (and actually quite desirable) change in weight distribution in favour of the back end.

A FRIENDLY RECEPTION

The GT was an instant hit with the press. Introducing the car in their '66 Models feature in October 1965, *Autocar* opened with the words: 'Perhaps one of the prettiest sports coupes ever to leave the BMC drawing boards is the new GT version of the MGB, which was released on the very eve of the Earls Court Show.' And they went on to hint at the GT's apparent versatility when they said: 'Whether it should be classed as a roomy coupe or as a potent estate car, it certainly combines the merits of both types.'

They still liked it when they did their first full road test, in March 1966, starting with the comment:

'One of the "hits" of last year's London Show, the new MGB GT coupe makes friends right away through its good looks and the exceptional practicality of its body. Perhaps there is more to its looks than simple beauty of form, for the car has an air of robust build and fitness for purpose which is borne out completely on the road . . . The quality of the interior furnishing and the care with which all the detail work has been planned put this GT well into the upper-middle class, so to speak . . .'

GT didn't escape the blight of the rubber bumper, even though the model was dropped from the US market shortly after they were introduced.

Thornley's 'managing director in the car park', in fact.

It *was* affordable, too – if not strictly speaking a 'poor man's Aston', or a poor man's anything else.

As launched, it was offered at £825, which with the addition of British purchase tax brought it tantalisingly below the £1,000 barrier, at £998.8.9d, or £143 more than the Roadster. Amazingly, that was also £52 *less* than the launch price of the A coupe nine years earlier!

Of course, as with the Roadster, that 'carrot' price tag for the B GT was just the start. The front anti-roll bar was standard and so was the oil cooler, but you still had to pay extra if you wanted a heater! That was

listed at £14.6.1d, overdrive was £60.8.4d, wire wheels were £30.4.2d (or £77.18.9d if you wanted chrome ones), Dunlop SP41 radial tyres to fit on them were £8.6.2d, Kangol seat belts (still only an option) were £3.5.0d each, fog lamps £4.9.6d each and a Radiomobile radio (with aerial and fitting) was £28.11.8d. Even wing mirrors were listed as an extra, at £1.7.7d.

Mechanically, apart from the different rear axle and the spring rates, the B GT (which had the five-bearing engine right from the start) was virtually identical to the Roadster, so it is no surprise that its performance was very similar. In fact, its extra weight (about 250lb) blunted the acceleration somewhat, but the more aerodynamic shape kept the top

Model: MGB GT   **Years:** 1965–1980

Body type: Two-plus-two GT, unitary construction
Engine type: Four-cylinder, in-line
Capacity: 1,798cc
Bore: 80.3mm
Stroke: 88.9mm
Compression ratio: 9.0:1
Cylinders: Cast-iron block, five main bearings
Cylinder head: Cast-iron, two valves per cylinder operated by pushrods
Fuel system: Twin SU carburettors
Maximum power: 97bhp @ 5,500rpm
Maximum torque: 105lb ft @ 2,500rpm
Bhp per litre: 53.9
Gearbox type: Four-speed manual, with overdrive
Gear ratios: Top: 1.00 (0.82o/d)   2nd: 2.17
                    3rd: 1.38 (1.13o/d)   1st: 3.40
Final drive ratio: 3.91
Clutch: Single dry plate
Front-suspension: Independent, by double wishbones, coil springs, lever arm
                        dampers, anti-roll bar
Rear-suspension: Live axle, semi-elliptic leaf springs, lever arm dampers
Brakes: Solid front discs, rear drums
Steering: Rack and pinion
Wheels & tyres: 5J×14in steel; 165SR14 Radial tyres
Overall length: 158.3in
Overall width: 61.8in
Overall height: 51.0in
Wheelbase: 91.0in
Track: Front: 49.0in   Rear: 49.3in
Ground clearance: 5.5in
Fuel tank capacity: 11 gallons
Unladen weight: 2,440lb
Power to weight ratio: 89.0bhp/ton

PERFORMANCE

Maximum speed: 100mph
0–60mph: 13.0 seconds
Standing ¼ mile: 19.0 seconds
Fuel consumption: 25mpg

speed up. *Autocar* managed 60mph (96.5kph) in 13.6 seconds (1.4 seconds slower than their first ever Roadster test) and 101mph (162kph) compared to 103mph, (165kph), but with the proviso that using the banked MIRA test track might have held top speed down a touch. *Motor*'s first GT tester was a shade quicker, at 13.2 seconds and 107mph (172kph), which was fairly typical.

Performance notwithstanding, of course, the GT did have that vestigial rear seat. It may only have been useful for very small children or one supple and transversely mounted adult, but it did allow the GT to be described as a '2 + 2' – and it did fold flat to make the newfound luggage space under the hatchback tail even more versatile.

Rear seat of the GT was strictly occasional, with little or no knee-room.

Vents in the bonnet of the GT.

THE GT IN PRODUCTION

And so the B GT's production career began. The first batch of shells was completely assembled by Pressed Steel, at a time when Roadster shells were still being finished in Coventry. Aside from that there were few differences in the assembly process, with all the elements finally coming together in Abingdon just as with the Roadster.

By the end of 1965, 524 GTs had been built, alongside that year's total of 24,179 Roadsters. The first full year of GT production added up to 10,241 cars, which put a small dent into Roadster production, which slipped slightly to 22,675. Happily for MG, the overall sales figure of almost 34,000 units showed that they weren't just converting sales from Roadster to GT, they genuinely had found an additional market. In the long term, almost exactly twenty-five per cent of Bs were GTs of one persuasion or another (and that later included the C GT and GT V8 derivatives).

As with the Roadster, sales on that level meant the GT initially far outstripped any rival in terms of volume – and it would be a little while yet before the Datsun 240Z (and its stodgier descendants) usurped the B's best-seller title in the early 1970s.

THE OPPOSITION

Looking back at that first *Autocar* test, the comparisons they chose were the Triumph TR4A, the Volvo P1800 and the Reliant Scimitar. All three were quicker than the GT in both top speed and 0–60 mph (0–96.5kph) acceleration, and only the glassfibre bodied Reliant was thirstier, but once again, the MG scored decisively on price. The Triumph was £1,011, the Reliant £1,292 and the rather esoteric Volvo was a whacking £1,814.

And even given all those options, there were still a few people who had their own ideas of what a B GT should look like. Probably the best of them was a lovely GT built on an early racing Roadster in 1967 by one Douglas Wilson-Spratt. Called the WSM, it had a handsome fastback line and a Kamm tail (like the Coune Berlinette). At the front it had a classically streamlined nose with faired-in headlamps which made it just a touch too long visually, but overall it looked not unlike various Ferraris. Wilson-Spratt originally planned to build his car in series, but 270 RBM remained an interesting one-off in the face of the production opposition.

By the time *Motor* carried a brief test on the recessed grille model B GT in October 1970, the alternatives had also expanded to include the Triumph TR6 and its stablemate the GT6, the Triumph-based Bond Equipe GT, the TVR Vixen, the Sunbeam Rapier and the Ford Capri 3000GT – surely as mixed a bag as you could wish to find anywhere.

Of this bunch, the GT fell pretty well midway in terms of maximum speed and acceleration, won fairly comfortably on fuel consumption, but was suddenly a lot less of a bargain. At £1,421 it undercut only the TR6 (at £1,515), being outpriced now by the big-engined Capri at £1,341, the Equipe at £1,284, the Rapier at £1,282, the GT6 at £1,272 and the TVR at a bargain basement £1,242.

The summing up, though, showed that, whatever the comparison, the B was still largely regarded as something unique: 'The MGB GT is still more refined sports car than genuine Grand Tourer. In some ways it is still unsophisticated and has a few detail faults – but even after eight years it's a very desirable package; the sales figures prove it'.

EARLY END IN THE USA

And so it continued to be, as the GT unfolded its career more or less in parallel with the Roadster, reflecting the same peaks of success and the same troughs of crisis. The 250,000th B, built in May 1971, was a US-

The 250,000th B off the Abingdon line was a left-hand drive
GT, in May 1971. Austin Morris's managing director George
Turnbull saw it off, alongside 'Old Number One'.

spec GT, but the coupe lasted only until 1975 on the US market.

It was withdrawn in the end, as outlined earlier, because its extra weight put it into a more stringent emissions class, which MG would have had a great deal of difficulty in meeting viably. As we shall see later, its demise in the States coincided with the arrival of the TR7 coupe, which raised the spectre of in-house politics once again, but the reality was that by that time the B was really just falling too far adrift of modern developments.

In the interim, it had, in general, shared its major revisions with the Roadster, as de-

tailed in the previous chapter — at least it had after 1967 when the Roadster caught up with the improved Salisbury axle spec and the floorpan changes that went with it.

As before, 1967 brought the 'MkII' and its all-synchro gearbox; 1969 saw the unpopular recessed grille on GTs as well as Roadsters; 1970 brought new seat materials for the US GT only; late 1972 saw the traditional grille reappear, plus a heated rear screen as standard (on GT only, obviously).

Even though the GT disappeared from the US market in 1975, it shared the 'Federal' rubber-bumper look from then on, for cost

saving through using common parts. That effectively meant that it was exempt from engine changes demanded by the US market, and the majority of the changes thereafter were strictly cosmetic: tinted glass late in 1976, for instance, and the 750-off limited edition 'Jubilee' model with special British Racing Green and gold livery in 1975, to celebrate the '50th anniversary' of the company.

And if that sounds rather negative, it isn't intended to be; the GT was a popular and versatile car that filled a specific niche very well and gave MG another best-selling line. In its fifteen-year run, over 125,000 GTs were built and the car in all its guises still has a faithful following of its own, quite different from the Roadster fraternity in many cases.

In the end, of course, the B GT suffered the same fate as the Roadster, and for much the same reasons – lack of development, lack of investment, pressure of legislation. By the late 1970s it was a sitting duck for the critics, and for the TR7 which British Leyland were all too obviously promoting to take its place.

In March 1980, *Car* magazine put the two – B GT and TR7 – together, 'to see if the B's demise, due in '81, is premature – or five years late'.

Their conclusion was pretty unequivocal: 'The Triumph is so clearly superior that you'd have to be crazy to buy an MG if your desire is a fast, good handling, comfortable sports coupe. The MG has even less to recommend it than we had thought it would at the outset of the test. It does not deserve still to be in the ranks of the new cars. In the company of the TR7 it seems merely a silly, irrelevant old car.'

By October, BL had finally bowed to the inevitable, too, and the GT, with the Roadster, was consigned to history.

7 The MGC

Give an enthusiast car engineer the bare bones of a basic model and the first thing he'll want to do is modify it – usually to make it quicker, better handling, more powerful: anything in fact to take it one step further than before. That's how Cecil Kimber got MG off the ground in the first place back in the early 1920s, and that's the philosophy that naturally enough still survived in Abingdon into the 1970s and even the 1980s, at least among the engineers.

So, once the B and the B GT were established as best-sellers in their own right, the MGC, as the next upgraded model would logically be called, was pretty well inevitable. All that space under the bonnet was far too big a temptation for anyone at MG to resist for very long, the only real question was what should be used to fill it.

CONSIDERING THE OPTIONS

That was a problem that had already been considered to some extent, even during the initial development of the car. There had been those 60 degrees V4 and V6 alternatives which had never progressed beyond the prototype stage, but which at least contributed to the finished design's conveniently wide bonnet opening. Later studies also included shoehorning all manner of strange alternatives under the B's bonnet, including the light but fragile Daimler V8 unit, the exceptionally attractive but really rather large Jaguar straight-six, the already outdated four-cylinder 2.7-litre lump from the Austin–Healey 100/4 and even a Coventry Climax V8 based on their racing engines.

Most tempting of all, of course (for BMC's accountancy bean-counters if not for MG's engineers), was the presence of the in-line six-cylinder Healeys in the corporate fold, which all too obviously gave another option for rationalisation. Even by the time the B appeared in 1962, BMC were looking quite seriously at a replacement for the steadily ageing Healey 3000 and it would have been very handy for the corporation to have had a big car that they could have badge engineered in something like the way they did with the Sprite and Midget. By 1963, ADO 51 and ADO 52 were the Austin–Healey and MG project versions of that car, with few differences other than the badging.

The catch with that was that part of what made the Healey a little long in the tooth was its 3-litre six-cylinder C-Series engine, a type which had originally appeared as long ago as 1954 to complete the A, B, C-Series family.

THE AUSTRALIAN CONNECTION

So part of the new project, in fact the major part, was to find an alternative engine, and once again BMC's innate conservatism had a great chance to shine through. The closest they actually got to adopting anything radically different for the new car was shortly after the B GT had appeared, when Abingdon built a one-off six-cylinder car using an Australian BMC engine.

That was the Australian-built 2,433cc 'Blue Flash' unit, which was normally used in cars like the Austin Freeway and the Wolseley 24/80. It wasn't an Australian version of the C-Series, it was actually more of a

Model: MGC & MGC GT   Years: 1967–1969

Body type: Two-seat open tourer and two-plus-two GT, unitary construction
Engine type: Six-cylinder, in-line
Capacity: 2,912cc
Bore: 83.3mm
Stroke: 88.9mm
Compression ratio: 9.0:1
Cylinders: Cast-iron block
Cylinder head: Cast-iron, two valves per cylinder operated by pushrods
Fuel system: Twin SU carburettors
Maximum power: 145bhp @ 5,250rpm
Maximum torque: 170lb ft @ 3,400rpm
Bhp per litre: 49.8
Gearbox type: Four-speed manual (overdrive optional, automatic optional)*
Gear ratios: Top: 1.00(0.82o/d)   2nd: 2.06   Reverse: 2.68
                   3rd: 1.31   1st: 2.98   (Manual, 3.31 drive &
                                                            o/d with 3.31)

Final drive ratio: 3.31:1 (Early cars 3.07:1, 3.70:1 with overdrive on later cars)
Clutch: Single dry plate, hydraulic operation
Front-suspension: Independent, by double wishbones, torsion bars, telescopic
                        dampers
Rear-suspension: Live axle, semi-elliptic leaf springs, lever arm dampers
Brakes: Solid front discs, rear drums
Steering: Rack and pinion
Wheels & tyres: 5J×15in steel or optional wire; 165×15in
Overall length: 153.3in
Overall width: 60.0in
Overall height: 50.0in
Wheelbase: 91.0in
Track: Front: 50.0in   Rear: 49.5in
Ground clearance: 5.5in
Fuel tank capacity: 12 gallons
Unladen weight: 2,460lb (Roadster), 2,610lb (GT)
Power to weight ratio: 132.0bhp/ton (Roadster), 124.4bhp/ton (GT)

PERFORMANCE

Maximum speed: 120mph
0–60mph: 10.0 seconds
Standing ¼ mile: 17.5 seconds
Fuel consumption: 19mpg

*Alternative Gear Ratios

	O/D	Top	3rd	2nd	1st	Reverse	Final Drive
Early Manual	—	1.00	1.38	2.17	3.44	3.09	3.07
Automatic	—	(=3rd)	1.00	1.45	2.39	2.09	3.31
Late Overdrive	0.82	1.00	1.31	2.06	2.98	2.68	3.70

six-cylinder B-Series — or one-and-a-half Bs together. It was lighter than the C-Series (which wouldn't have been difficult) and in the B shell, with three SU carbs, it was apparently potent enough to have Roy Brocklehurst timed through a police speed trap at a rather naughty 127mph (204kph).

That was the good side, the bad side was that it would have had to have been shipped half way round the world if it was to be used by MG; and, good as the Blue Flash was, it was as good as it was likely to get — it had simply reached the limits of its development.

In the end, therefore, there was the inevitable compromise, and like the B before it, the C inherited what was actually an engine destined for another of BMC's Austin saloons — in this case, the big (and ultimately unsuccessful) Austin 3-litre, ADO 61.

A HEAVYWEIGHT SOLUTION

The updated C-Series that BMC had developed for the forthcoming rear-drive saloon had the same dimensions as the earlier C-Series, at 83.4×88.9mm bore and stroke, for a capacity of 2,912cc. Most of the work had gone into the crankshaft area, in much the same way as the 1,800 B-Series engine which the B adopted had been upgraded for the Austin 1800.

Again, the object of the redesign was to improve refinement and reliability — not to give more power. For the saloon, there were seven main bearings instead of the previous four, which dictated both narrower mains and a repositioning of the bore centres. Where the B-Series for the 1800 and the B had moved its bores so close together as to lose most of the cooling passages between them, the new C-Series for the 3-litre saloon and the C took advantage of the new bottom end (and the better thin-wall casting techniques) to split its three pairs of siamesed cylinders, and in the process it *gained* some water passages between cylinders.

It also had a heavily revised cylinder head, with relocated combustion chambers and, most importantly, the ability to accept emission control additions when necessary — meaning the car should have no problems in meeting foreseeable US requirements. The US market cars used a different alloy inlet manifold with separate air cleaners rather than the big, single type of UK market cars, and they had an air-injection system with a power-sapping engine-driven AC Delco air pump. As for more minor changes, the new engine now had a negative earth electrical system with alternator charging, and a pre-engaged starter motor.

A WEIGHTY PROBLEM

Unfortunately for John Thornley and his team, the combination of new head design and more internal friction meant that the

The bonnet bulge and slightly larger wheels gave the C a very much chunkier look than the B even though the external changes were relatively minor.

new engine produced marginally *less* power than its C-Series predecessor. In the saloon it was rated at just 118bhp, on an 8.2:1 compression ratio and fairly mild cam. For the MG application, it amounted to 145bhp at 5,250rpm and a torque peak of 170lb ft at 3,400rpm, running on a compression ratio of 9.0:1 and a pair of SU HS6 carbs. And worse, far worse, was that although it had become externally a little more compact after its redesign, it wasn't nearly as light as Coventry had promised him it was going to be – and that was the nub of all the C's subsequent problems.

Years later, Thornley put it in a nutshell: 'The MGC's engine was about half a hundredweight too heavy. If we could have got it down to the design weight, we'd have had a world-beater.'

As it was, although the engine was more than half as powerful again as the four-cylinder B's, and had over half as much torque again, it was also more than 200lb heavier. Thornley had been promised that it would be more than 70lb lighter than it turned out to be . . .

Inevitably, that meant some last minute rethinking, because by the time the first engines arrived at Abingdon, in 1965, the car to put them in was virtually complete, having been built around the promised dimensions of the new unit, but obviously not its final weight.

That chassis re-engineering had been largely the province of Roy Brocklehurst, and his job had been considerably more complex than might at first be suggested by just swapping a four for a six.

His main problem in re-engineering the front of the B shell for the new engine was in physically getting it to go in. He was helped a little bit in that by the engine having lost about 1¾in (4.5cm) from its length (without which it probably wouldn't have gone in at all), but it was still a tight squeeze, both longitudinally and vertically.

The longitudinal problem was solved by re-siting the radiator as far forward as it would possibly go, and losing the B's familiar diaphragm radiator mount, which would have been somewhere around the middle of number one cylinder! The new, sealed cooling system had its radiator right up against the transverse front panel which carried the bonnet catch – and the bonnet itself had to be modified to clear it, of which more in a moment.

The C also had an all-new, all-synchro gearbox (which could also be fitted with the usual overdrive unit as an option, in which case it had very slightly different internal ratios). Like the engine, it came courtesy of the new 3-litre saloon programme, and it was adopted in modified form for the B (which became the MkII) at the same time as the C was eventually launched.

The Borg Warner automatic option appeared on the C too, right from its launch – being offered on the B MkII from the same time, as previously outlined.

Unfortunately for the engineers, both the new all-synchro gearbox and the automatic were larger than the earlier three-synchro box with which the B had been launched, and that meant that the six-cylinder engine and gearbox assembly couldn't be pushed any further back into the car, even with major modifications, without losing an unacceptable amount of passenger space. It would also have meant moving the heater unit and probably the brake servo. Even so, some re-engineering of the transmission tunnel and front bulkhead were necessary to accommodate either the new all-synchro gearbox or the automatic, and those changes were carried over to subsequent B shells to rationalise those parts.

CHANGING TO TORSION BARS

Having squeezed the six-cylinder engine in longitudinally, Brocklehurst now faced an

even bigger problem in getting it to fit vertically. The problem was that, even with the
main depth of the sump pan moved a long
way back, it was just too deep to work with
the original front crossmember which carries
the coil spring and wishbone front-
suspension on the B.

The solution was to replace the removable
crossmember with a completely redesigned
fixed type and to replace the coil spring
suspension with torsion bars. The new crossmember was rather less substantial than the
old detachable type, which meant that there
was no way it could take the coil spring loads,
and it was shaped to come up alongside the
sides of the new engine to where it was fixed
to the new inner wing panels. Instead of having to take the spring loads at its upper ends,
it now only had to take damper loads and the
dampers were changed from the old lever
type to the more modern telescopic type,
whose upper ends can be seen under the bonnet roughly where the top mounts of the B
crossmember would have been.

ADJUSTABLE

On each side, the telescopic damper now
passed between the arms of a very wide top
wishbone, while the lower wishbone was
replaced by a substantial single link which
attaches to the front end of the long torsion
bars. The bars run back, parallel to the
centre line of the car and just to either side of
the transmission tunnel, to adjustable
mountings carried in a new and heavy crossmember underneath the shell in a position
just under the seats.

A front anti-roll bar was standard right
from the word go on the C, and it was a
slightly thicker one than the one that was
used on the B. The floorpan was also generally beefed up in many areas, which made
the C shell somewhat stiffer than the B's but
also a good deal heavier, to add to the
engine's contribution.

LOSING BALANCE

The net result of all these changes was that
weight went up by some 400lb over the B
(about half from the new engine and half
from the chassis changes) and the vast
majority of it went over the front axle. The
weight distribution therefore changed from
the B's approximately 52/48 balance to a
substantially more nose heavy 56/44 front
bias. This prompted MG to change the ratio
of the repositioned steering rack, settling for
a lighter but less responsive three and a half
turns between locks instead of the B's three,
and to increase the road wheel size by an
inch, from 14in (35.5cm) to 15in (38cm).

The semi-elliptic rear-suspension layout
stayed essentially unchanged from the B, but
with a stronger Salisbury tubular axle and
slightly stiffer springs to cope with the added
weight. The brakes were uprated, too – with
larger Girling discs at the front (in place of
the B's Lockheeds) and smaller diameter but
wider drums at the rear.

From the outside, the only visual clues
were the slightly taller ride height on the
bigger wheels, and the aforementioned bonnet bulge, which comprised the large hump
to clear the radiator and the front of the
engine, plus a small blip halfway down the
left-hand side to clear the dashpot of the forward SU carb. The bonnet was still in aluminium by the time the C arrived, and stayed
that way until its demise.

From the inside, there was even less to distinguish the C from the B, the straight
(rather than slightly cranked) gearlever
became commonised with the D and the only
other difference was that the C gained a
neatly leather covered steering wheel rim.

And now the C was on its own. Between the
first prototype in 1965 and the C's launch in
1967, a short run of pre-production cars had
been built during 1966. Part of the reason for
those was to finalise details including the
'badge engineering' of the putative Austin–
Healey version, but that car never appeared.

*3-litre 150bhp straight-six was a tight fit under the B's bonnet,
necessitating the far forward radiator position and redesign of
the front-suspension, with torsion bars.*

Like the four-cylinder engine, C's big six uses twin SU carbs with inlets on the same side as the exhausts: most of the underbonnet furniture is basically familiar.

Healey founder Donald, and his son Geoffrey, weren't impressed by the C, and although they knew that the Healey 3000 was to be phased out by 1967, they declined to have their name on the new car, which with hindsight was not a wholly bad decision.

Their biggest worry was the new engine, which they already knew was a major disappointment. It was so bad that it even led to the scheme to revive the old *four*-cylinder engine, as used in the Healey 100. The block was still in production (it was used in taxis!) and BMC looked at the feasibility of engineering new cranks and a twin-cam cylinder head, which they calculated should give something between 160 and 180bhp. Even at that, they hoped they might still have made the engine more cheaply than the new six.

The Healeys would then have been rather more enthusiastic about having a four-cylinder car with their name on it that would out-perform the six-cylinder one with the MG badge. Predictably enough, it was never allowed to happen and the Healeys reverted to plans to enlarge the 3000, while Abingdon made the most of what they were stuck with.

EXTENDING THE FAMILY

So, when the MGC took its first bow, at the 1967 London Motor Show in October, it was purely MG. It was offered in both Roadster and GT guise, extending the family to four- and six-cylinder Roadsters and four- and six-cylinder GTs, which ought really to have given MG's sales managers some cause for optimism. The C, after all, promised considerably better performance than the B and, what's more, it was extremely competitively priced; at £1,011 the Roadster was only £153

The C was launched in both Roadster and GT body variants, and sold in virtually equal numbers in the model's three-year production run.

more than the equivalent B and the £1,249 GT was just £155 more than the B GT.

And then the press got their hands onto it and their teeth into it.

Basically, they could barely find a good word for the C between them. It was quick enough in a straight line, at 120mph (193kph) for the Roadster which *Autocar* tested shortly after its launch, and with a 0–60mph (0–96.5kph) time of ten seconds dead in the same test; but that was about the only good thing that anybody could say about it.

The big problem (and even allowing for the press's natural tendency never to allow a chance to have a gripe go by unrewarded, it was a *real* problem) was all that weight up front.

In spite of Brocklehurst's (and Enever's and Thornley's) best efforts, it had lost the idiot-proof poise and lightness of touch of the B and become a ponderous and lifeless under-steerer. The lower geared steering had failed to compensate fully for the extra weight, while becoming less sharp and communicative, and they didn't even like the new engine.

The comparison with the outgoing (and still much loved) big Healey was inevitable, and the C lost it hands downs; the performance was actually very similar on paper, but the new engine had none of the responsive feel or even the noise of the old Healey 3000 unit (which, incidentally, ended its run with an output of 148bhp, albeit in a slightly heavier car). The best anyone could think of to say about the C was generally along the lines that it would make a good high speed tourer, but considering that MG had set out to create a sports car to outrun the B (and a GT closer to Thornley's original 'poor man's Aston' theme), it was damning with faint praise.

What's more, there was precious little that Abingdon could do about it, at least not within their usual budgetary constraints; the

As before, steel wheels were original equipment on the C, but most buyers preferred optional wires to the plain look.

Larger wheels and slightly increased ride height are evident enough if you look closely.

combined problems of unwanted weight and the disappointing engine were really too fundamental. They compensated a little for the lifeless mid-range acceleration in 1968, by lowering the rear axle ratio (except on the auto-equipped cars) to make the most of the really rather inadequate torque and to put a bit more pep into the acceleration. The internal gearbox ratios were also standardised between ordinary and overdrive cars, adopting the closer ratios of the original overdrive type.

NOT ENOUGH

It was all to very little avail. The C just never caught on, and as the next metamorphosis of BMC into British Leyland brought its own problems, the C fizzled towards an early demise.

That came in September 1969, when the last car, a left-hand-drive GT, left Abingdon. It left the total output of Cs in the model's twenty-six-month production run at just one car short of 9,000. Of those, 4,550 were Roadsters and 4,449 were GTs. As ever, America had been the biggest market, buy-

ing 4,256 Cs of one kind or another, while only 3,437 found homes in Britain.

There was one late fling for the C, when a batch of unsold cars were bought by London MG dealers University Motors, given cosmetic changes including a rather ugly new grille with horizontal bars and matt black surround, and sold as University Motors MG Specials. Most of them also had engine modifications by the enormously respected Wiltshire tuning firm of Downton, whose founder, Daniel Richmond, was also one of Britain's most successful Mini and B tuners.

University sold something over 150 cars in the two years after the C's official demise – the vast majority of them being GTs.

WHAT MIGHT HAVE BEEN?

In all honesty, there was very little sadness at the passing of the C and very little surprise, but there had been just one sign of what the C might have been with more development. That was a very short series of very special Cs which were built *before* the C appeared in production, early in 1967.

The main bonnet bulge accommodates a long engine and forward mounted radiator, the blip on the side clears forward SU carb.

By that time, BMC's Abingdon-based Competitions Department was looking for a successor to the big Healey for sports car racing and for rallying. They obviously saw the basic tool for the job in the forthcoming six-cylinder C. The lightweight shells on which the planned racers would have been based were built by Pressed Steel, using a good deal of alloy panelling but retaining the necessary stiffness.

In the end, only six of these lightweight cars, properly known as the MGC GTS, were built, two of them assembled by the works and raced briefly until the latest regime again pulled the plug on any racing activity; the other four 'unofficial' cars were assembled later by British-based racing enthusiast John Chatham — two of them as racers and two as something closer to the sort of road car that the C should have been in the first place.

We will look at their story in a lot more detail when we outline the B's racing history, but suffice it to say for now that they were later described as being many of the things the C never was: civilised, tractable, light and precise, with smooth flexibility from any revs.

MG certainly couldn't have got away with building anything obviously so close to outright racing cars as the GTS for the road even if they could have afforded to at the time, but maybe the GTS does suggest that there was a glimmer of hope for the C had the management wanted and been prepared to pay for it.

As things were, it would be another three and a half years before MG had another (and this time very much more successful) go at building a bigger engined B, the excellent but sadly under-exploited V8.

8 The MGB GT V8

Of all the if-only stories in the history of the B, the if-only of the B GT V8 is probably the biggest. With the lightweight 3.5-litre Rover V8 engine nestling comfortably in the nose of the B GT, with ample power and none of the C's terminal nose-heaviness, the V8 was a gem of a car. Even though the whole B concept was getting on in years by the time it was launched, in 1973, the V8 had the potential to bring the B right back into the front line, and unlike the B- and C-Series engines that had preceded it, it had the scope for a huge amount of continued development left in it.

But it survived for just three and a half years until it was unceremoniously dropped from the range after a total of just 2,591 cars had been built. There was never a Roadster version of the V8 (not from the works, at least) and it was never exported to the USA – even though that might have seemed like its natural habitat and it was originally intended that up to fifty per cent of production should cross the Atlantic.

When that didn't happen, US emission control requirements were one of the problems cited, of course; volume supply of engines was another – the management line being that they simply didn't have the resources to produce V8 engines for both Rover and MG. And without the US market, the car was never going to be viable.

Those of a more cynical nature might have looked at the simultaneous rise of the new Triumph TR7 and the decline of the B; and they might have raised a wry smile at the introduction of the TR8 to the USA (complete with the 'hard-to-get, impossible-to-detox' Rover engine) not so very long after the total cancellation of the B GT V8.

SUCCESSOR WITHOUT SUCCESS

But that was the end, the beginnings were in the very early 1970s, when the MG company were clearly in need of something to replace the unfortunate C for the 'big-engined-B' marketplace.

For the factory, first thoughts of the V8-engined B began around 1970, by which time both the Rover and Triumph (as in Stag) V8 engines had been appraised. Of course, by this time all of these options were in the family, so to speak; the previously independent Rover company had been absorbed into the Leyland fold in 1967, alongside Triumph, which had been there since 1961, and in 1968 the Leyland Motor Corporation had merged with British Motor Holdings (BMH née BMC, and including MG) to form the British Leyland Motor Corporation.

Ultimately, as we've seen, Triumph predominated, but there was at least a honeymoon period for MG.

One of the gems that Rover brought into the fold, of course, was its V8 engine – or rather the V8 engine that it had adopted as its own in the mid 1960s.

The compact all-alloy unit had actually originated as a General Motors (GM) unit in the USA, in 1961, when it was used in the Buick Special, the Pontiac Tempest and the Oldsmobile F-85. Rover had acquired the rights to build the engine under licence after GM had stopped using it around 1963; its expensive aluminium construction had effectively been rendered redundant there by cheaper cast-iron engines using the latest thin-wall casting techniques which had also played their part in the original 1,800 B

As launched, in August 1973, the GT V8 predated the rubber bumper era . . .

engine.

Rover themselves, ironically, pulled out of the US market during the 1960s, so they never needed to de-tox the engine to take it back there. Instead, it first appeared in Britain in 1967, in the big P5/P6 saloons and Coupes – and that was the same year that the ill-fated MGC had made its first appearance. Later, it went on to power cars as diverse as the Range Rover and the TVR, plus some spectacularly quick Rovers including the SD1 Vitesse derivatives which brought Rover considerable racing success well into the late 1980s.

AN IDEAL ENGINE

The all-alloy, single-cam, pushrod overhead-valve engine is a lazy, low stressed unit with a tremendous reputation for being reliable and long-lived – its only real weakness being a tendency for the hydraulic tappets to become a bit tired after 60,000 miles or so. Virtually the only thing that Rover changed in bringing the engine to Europe was the carburation, from the American Rochester to the inevitable British SUs.

With bore and stroke dimensions of 88.9 × 71.1mm (that's 3.5x2.8in) for a capacity of

. . . but they soon caught up with this model just as with the rest of the range, even though it was never sold in the USA.

3,528cc, and a comfortable potential for a spread of power choices on either side of 150bhp, it was a natural choice for MG. It was bigger, lighter and simpler than the Triumph alternative, and a lot less encum-bered by political implications, and it has since proved itself far more of a survivor than the modern but temperamental Triumph V8.

MG weren't quite the first sports car people to spot its potential. Morgan adopted it for

Although the V8 was a tight squeeze under the B's bonnet, the installation problems were marginally less severe than they had been with the long and heavy six for the C.

their traditional looking but staggeringly quick Plus 8, early in 1968, appropriately enough when supplies of the Triumph TR4A engine dried up. Production of the Rover-engined Morgan ended only very recently.

And before MG managed to get their own car to market, a one time Mini racer from Farnborough in Kent beat them to it.

THE COSTELLO V8

He was Ken Costello, proprietor of Costello Motor Engineering Ltd, and he started marketing his car in 1970, at more or less the same time as MG started work on their own version. He launched it by letting a group of journalists from Britain's national news-

papers and the specialist press have brief drives and their enthusiastic comments brought Costello to the public eye with a vengeance, which must have been slightly embarrassing for MG.

He wasn't quite so enthusiastic about having his early cars subjected to the punishment of a full magazine road test, though, and that didn't happen until 1972. The reticence, it seems, was because the standard B gearbox that he used was a weak link when abused.

That was not too surprising, Costello's car used a more powerful version of the V8 than MG would ultimately adopt, and a more powerful version than Rover themselves were then offering. Rover's basic engine then produced 144bhp at 5,000rpm and 197lb ft of

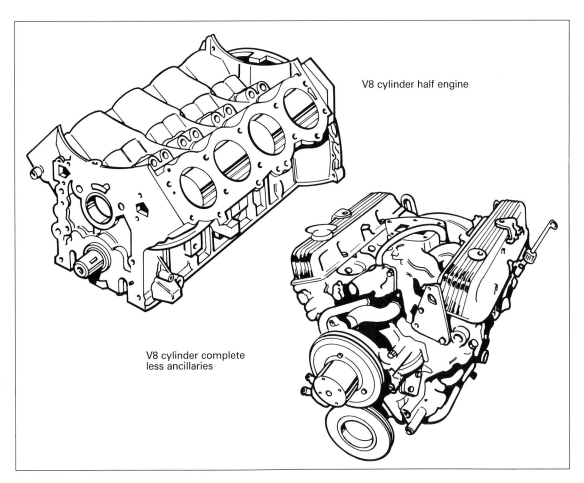

V8 cylinder half engine

V8 cylinder complete
less ancillaries

*The V8 was little longer than the B's original four-cylinder
engine, actually lighter than the four and far lighter than the
six-cylinder C engine.*

torque; in their 3500S, with better exhaust manifolding, it gave 150bhp and 204lb ft, at the same respective revs.

Initially, Costello fitted the engine in absolutely standard form, with Rover's crossover SU carburettor arrangement in the centre of the block, which meant his car had to have a fairly large bonnet bulge. Later cars had a Weber carb, plus skimmed cylinder heads, a lighter flywheel and a balanced crank – in which form it was claimed to give 185bhp.

To go with that, he fitted the stronger MGC propshaft, and a modified steering column with two Hooke joints instead of one. British Leyland apparently disapproved of that on safety grounds, but Costello was happy that it was perfectly adequate, and it allowed him a bit more flexibility in exhaust manifold design.

He also planned to produce his own five-speed gearbox (with Hewland internals) but that was overtaken by the launch of the 'official' B GT V8 in 1973, which effectively rendered the Costello V8 pointless. It had been a good car, but it was an expensive one too, at £2,443 in 1972, when the B GT on

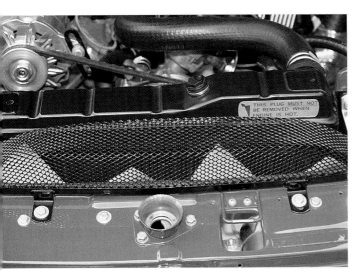

The radiator didn't need to be so far forward for the V8.

which it was based cost just £1,459. On top of that you could also pay extra for overdrive and for the attractive alloy wheels (similar to the ones that eventually appeared on the works car, but not the same), which put the price up to over £2,500.

Costello's problems had actually started before Abingdon produced their own V8, when his official line of engine supply from BL dried up, but there was no suggestion that they cut off the supply for any reason other than that they simply didn't have enough engines for their own needs.

In any case, by June 1973 *Motor* were hinting that some serious competition was just round the corner, when they remarked in a rare full test of the Costello car: 'Rumour has it that Ken C won't be the only man in the MGB V8 conversion for very much longer, so

The manifolding for twin SU carbs looked strange but worked well and allowed MG to keep the smooth bonnet line.

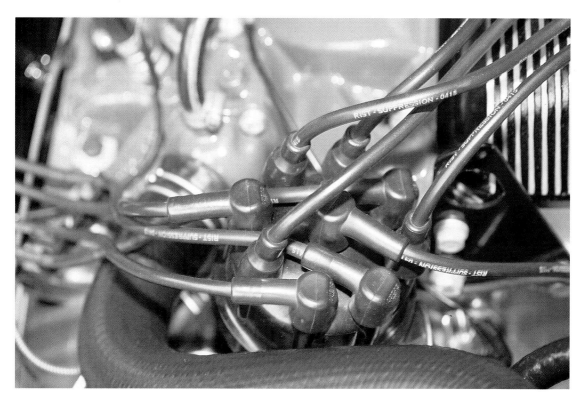

Eight leads from the V8 distributor – spark plug connections occasionally give problems.

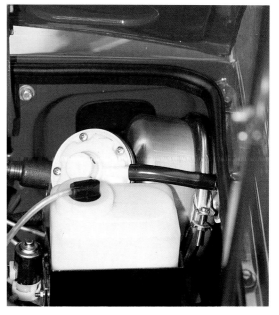

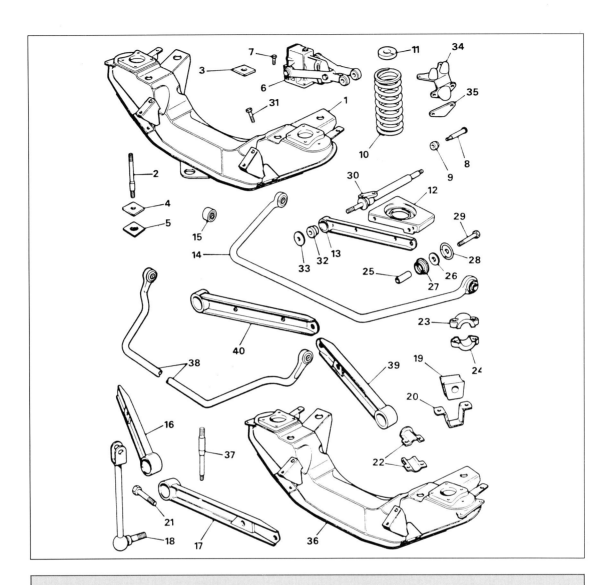

1 Crossmember	10 Spring-coil	19 Bearing-anti-roll bar	30 Pivot-wishbone
2 Bolt-crossmember to body	11 Spigot-spring	20 Strap-bearing	31 Bolt-pivot to member
3 Pad-mounting-upper	12 Seat-spring	21 Bolt-anti-roll bar to link	32 Bush-wishbone arm
4 Pad-mounting-lower	13 Arm-wishbone	22 Stop-end location	33 Washer-retaining
5 Plate-clamp	14 Bar assembly-anti-roll	23 Bar assembly-anti-roll	34 Buffer-rebound
6 Absorber-shock	15 Bush	24 Locator-lower	35 Piece-distance
7 Bolt	16 Arm-wishbone-front-RH	25 Tube-distance-link	36 Crossmember-front
8 Pin-fulcrum-link to shock absorber arm	17 Arm-wishbone-front-LH	26 Washer-thrust-link	37 Bolt-mounting
9 Bearing-fulcrum pin	18 Link anti-roll bar	27 Seal-link	38 Bar assembly-anti-roll
		28 Support	39 Arm-wishbone-front
		29 Bolt-wishbone to link	40 Arm-wishbone-rear

Where the C had been obliged to use torsion bar front suspension to accommodate extra weight, B GT V8 was able to revert to familiar coil springs and lever dampers, with anti-roll bar.

there may be an interesting comparison for us to report on soon . . .'

THE OFFICIAL ALTERNATIVE

Abingdon, of course, had seen Costello's car at a very early stage, in 1971. When he was asking for further engine supplies and even looking to offer warranties with his cars, he was asked to show it to MG chief engineer Roy Brocklehurst for his approval (or otherwise). Brocklehurst did identify a few details that he thought needed changing, and it's fairly clear that Leyland decided there and then that if they could advise Costello on his car, they could equally well build their own.

The story then goes that their own first prototype was completed within twenty-eight days (albeit with a Costello-style bonnet bulge to clear the standard carb mountings) and was well enough received to get the go-ahead for production development – including re-engineering the carb layout to allow a standard bonnet line. The solution to that one was a completely new secondary manifold between the usual cast device in the centre of the vee and the carbs, which were now at the back of the engine, facing the bulkhead. They were fed their air through a single flat air box, from either end of which an air cleaner extended over each rocker cover. From forward of the air cleaners, each intake ran down to an opening near its respective exhaust manifold, controlled by a clever BL device, a patented shut-off flap controlled by bi-metal strips. These were designed to help the engine meet European ECE 15 exhaust emission regulations, especially when the engine was cold and therefore running at its dirtiest. They could either divert the air over the exhaust system to feed the engine with pre-heated air, or when it was up to running temperature could move the flaps and draw colder air directly from under the bonnet.

The oil filter was moved into series with the oil cooler pipework instead of in the base of the pump, and there was a larger radiator, plus an AC Delco alternator and two thermostatically controlled electric fans, ahead of the radiator.

Again, the modifications didn't take very long, and BL didn't plan to spend too much money on the V8 – the estimates for tooling were originally just £250,000.

There were underbonnet sheet metal changes to be made around the inner wings and the front bulkhead, there was the new carburettor and manifold layout plus the other minor engine changes and the re-siting for the radiator, but there were none of the major chassis changes that had been necessary for the C.

The very first production car was actually built in December 1972, and a few left-hand drive cars were built very early in 1973, for evaluation for the US market. There was then something of a hiatus until series production started in April 1973, during which time the plans for a US version had been dropped. As the original plan was for a production rate of around a hundred cars a week with fifty per cent earmarked for the USA, that was quite a big decision, officially prompted by engine availability problems rather than by any inability to meet Federal regulations.

AN EXPENSIVE ALTERNATIVE

So, MG launched the real thing in August 1973, at £2,294 compared to the current £1,547 for the B GT. It was offered only in right-hand drive and only as a GT, because Abingdon felt that the B Roadster shell was not quite strong enough for V8 power, especially around the scuttle. Brocklehurst also suggested that the Roadster was more sensitive to wheel and tyre equipment and so the V8 was never tried in the Roadster shell – at

Model: MGB GT V8   **Years:** 1973–1976

Body type: Two-plus-two GT, unitary construction
Engine type: V8, 90 degree
Capacity: 3,528cc
Bore: 88.9mm
Stroke: 71.1mm
Compression ratio: 8.25:1
Cylinders: Aluminium alloy block, five main bearings
Cylinder heads: Aluminium alloy, two valves per cylinder, operated by pushrods
Fuel system: Twin SU carburettors
Maximum power: 137bhp @ 5,000rpm
Maximum torque: 193lb ft @ 2,900rpm
Bhp per litre: 38.8
Gearbox type: Four-speed manual, overdrive on top gear
Gear ratios: Top: 1.00 (0.82 o/d)   2nd: 1.97   Reverse: 2.82
                  3rd: 1.26   1st: 3.14
Final drive ratio: 3.07:1
Clutch: Single dry plate, hydraulic actuation
Front-suspension: Independent, by double wishbones, coil springs, lever arm
                        dampers, anti-roll bar
Rear-suspension: Live axle, semi-elliptic leaf springs, lever arm dampers
Brakes: Solid front discs, rear drums
Steering: Rack and pinion
Wheels & tyres: Composite: alloy centres/steel rims, 5J×14in;
                      175HR14 Radial tyres
Overall length: 154.7in
Overall width: 60.0in
Overall height: 50.0in
Wheelbase: 91.0in
Track: Front: 49.0in   Rear: 49.3in
Ground clearance: 4.5in
Fuel tank capacity: 12 gallons
Unladen weight: 2,390lb
Power to weight ratio: 128.4bhp/ton

PERFORMANCE

Maximum speed: 125mph
0–60mph: 8.5 seconds
Standing ¼ mile: 16.5 seconds
Fuel consumption: 22mpg

*Minor interior changes on the V8 included smaller speedo and
solid-spoked leather-rimmed wheel.*

least not by the works. The one person who
tried that was the same John Chatham who
had built the 'non-works' lightweight Cs. His
car was based on the C Roadster, with a
Costello V8, straight-cut gears with competition overdrive on third and fourth, and competition suspension and brakes. It sat on 7×
14in (18x36cm) Minilite wheels with big
Goodyear G800 tyres and it was capable of
reaching 60mph (96.5kph) in less than six
seconds or, given a longer axle ratio, going on
to around 140mph (225kph). With an almost
standard body it must have handed out quite
a few serious frights.

MG themselves might have put the new

engine into the rather stronger C Roadster
body, of course, but they didn't even try; the
production V8 was always based firmly on
the coil-spring suspended B shell and there
was never any intention of resurrecting the
torsion bar suspended C chassis as a basis. In
any case, with no US market to satisfy, having a Roadster was of considerably less
importance; by the early 1970s the UK
market was far more interested in closed cars
with a bit more refinement.

To a degree, the B GT V8 gave them what
they wanted, but it wasn't received by the
press with anything like the sort of enthusiasm that might have been expected. In the

Roy Brocklehurst

Roy Brocklehurst, the man who designed so much of the B's mechanical layout, was born in 1932, the son of a miner. He joined MG straight from school in 1947, at the age of fifteen, going to work for Syd Enever as a design apprentice.

Enever, characteristically, threw him in at the deep end, and he was set to drawing some new valvegear and a special crank-shaft for Enever's beloved Gardner record breaker.

In 1952 he left to complete two years National Service with the RAF, and return-ed to Abingdon in June 1954 (the year in which the design office re-opened) as a design draughtsman. In 1956 he became chief draughtsman, and it was in that capacity that he worked on the B.

He also worked on the A, of course, on all the subsequent record breakers, on the GT, C, and the V8, plus all the prototypes that didn't make it.

When Enever retired in 1971, he became chief engineer. He once voiced his frustra-tion on all the legislation that governed that job: 'Nowadays, you don't design a motor car any more – you just throw up all the regula-tions and draw a line around them'.

As MG was wound down, Brocklehurst was snapped up by the main BL organisa-tion and he went to Longbridge to help develop the Metro, Maestro and Montego. In 1981 he became chief engineer of BL Technology Ltd at their huge new research facility at Gaydon. He took early retirement in 1988, but died, tragically and suddenly, in April that year.

V8's case it wasn't a hatchet job on the scale of that applied to the C, more a studied indif-ference.

Part of the problem, perhaps, was that the V8 had been too long anticipated, and a lot of people were expecting too much of the new car.

As it was, what they got was something that had few external changes from the four-cylinder GT. It had rather nice alloy-centred, steel rimmed wheels (originally seen shortly before on a safety-orientated exercise on the GT, the SSV1) with slightly bigger tyres the usual 14in (36cm) diameter, but slightly chunkier with a 175 section. The ride height was an inch higher, not just because of the tyres but also because the V8 had suspension changes anticipating the forthcoming US requirements which would reach full frui-tion in the rubber bumper cars; and there were discreet V8 badges on the grille, the left front wing and the tailgate. They were pinched from the Rover V8.

Maybe the hacks were expecting some-thing more like the lightweight C racers, the GTS, with big wheelarches and a touch of flamboyance, maybe even a tell-tale hump on the bonnet, at the very least a new grille. If they were, no wonder they were dis-appointed.

There were few changes inside, either; the main instruments were slightly smaller (to comply with American regulations, though that turned out to be rather superfluous), and the numbers were different to reflect the dif-ferent engine and performance, but that was about all.

Even under the skin, the changes were minimal. The suspension was slightly up-rated at both ends, but only to the extent of stiffer springs. The Lockheed front disc brakes were made thicker (up from 0.35 to 0.5in (0.8–1cm)). The B's optional brake servo was fitted as standard, and there was a bigger clutch, driving a gearbox essentially based on the C's internals – with overdrive as stan-dard. The bigger clutch, to cope with the addi-tional power and torque, had demanded a bigger bellhousing, too. On the earliest cars the overdrive operated on both third and top gear, but soon it was changed to top gear only.

THE REAL CHANGE

The big change, of course, was in the engine. MG had resisted going the whole hog and lift-

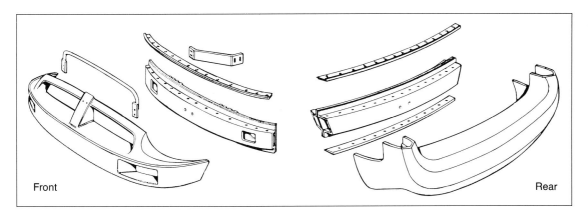

There was a lot more to the new bumpers than just an unsightly rubber shell; substantial underpinnings added a considerable amount of weight.

ing the most potent of the V8s from Rover; again with emission rules in mind, they had opted for an 8.25:1 compression ratio instead of the saloon's 10.5:1, but at least that meant the B GT V8 would run on three-star petrol – and that was quite important with the 'energy crisis' just around the corner.

There was still enough power increase to be worthwhile. Where the four-cylinder had offered 95bhp, the V8 as adapted for the B gave 137bhp at 5,000rpm – an increase of just over forty-four per cent. The torque improvement was even more spectacular, up from 110lb ft at 3,000rpm to 193lb ft at an even more slogging 2,900rpm – or an increase of more than seventy-five per cent.

What's more, none of these increases was at the expense of either weight or balance – the twin disasters in the MGC equation.

Without their ancillaries, the all-alloy V8 was 40lb *lighter* than the cast iron four-cylinder B-Series (and an amazing 240lb lighter than the six cylinder C!). With its extra bits and pieces, it was marginally heavier than the four, but it was mounted a long way back under the bonnet to give weight distribution that was as close to 50/50 as any B variant ever achieved. As it turned out, most testers thought that was not quite as delicate as the four-cylinder B's 48/52, but there was no suggestion that the V8 had any of the C's dire problems.

In fact the finished car weighed in at 167lb more than the four-cylinder, which meant that the power to weight ratio went up from 109bhp per ton to 126bhp per ton, an increase of just short of sixteen per cent, where many testers might have been expecting a bit more, given the power in the Rover saloons.

INTO A DIFFERENT LEAGUE

Nevertheless, they could hardly complain of a lack of performance. *Autocar*'s first test, in August 1973, reported a top speed of 124mph (199kph) and a 0–60mph (0–96.5kph) time of 8.6 seconds – a very far cry from the four-cylinder's bare 100mph (160kph) and 12 or so seconds to the yardstick 60. *Motor Sport* reported almost exactly the same figures, except that Clive Richardson noted, on one gentle downhill stretch of autoroute during his French drive story, seeing the speedo needle 'playing somewhere around the imaginary 150mph mark and the rev counter into the red, before realisation struck home and the throttle was lifted rapidly'.

Notwithstanding the newfound performance, though, most testers inevitably kept referring back to the vintage nature of what was underneath, *Autocar* again:

Attractive alloy wheels were introduced for the V8, used on later special editions. Rubber bumpers appeared in October 1974.

'If the end product falls short in any way, it is in the unfortunate perpetuation of the dated features of the MGB. Such shortcomings as excessive wind noise, a harsh ride and heavy steering may be forgiven in an out-and-out sports car, but they have no place in a GT car costing over £2,000. More unfortunate still is the fact that such shortcomings are accentuated by the superb smoothness and relative quietness of the excellent Rover V8 engine . . .'

MG must have wondered what they *did* have to do to please their critics, but at least one of those moans, the one about price, was perhaps unnecessarily self-inflicted. At its launch price of £2,293.96p (with the only extra being seat belts at £15.85), the MGB GT V8 was selling for a lot more than it actually needed to. It may have been that BL were convinced by the Costello's modest suc-

cess at a similar price that people *would* pay quite handsomely for a V8. Or it may just have been that they knew that the model would never sell in anything more than tiny numbers and that even recovering the limited development costs would require a substantial profit per unit.

Ford, of course, set about the market in rather a different way with the low-price, high-volume Capri that was one of the GT V8's most damaging competitors. The full four-seater, 122mph (196kph) Capri 3000GXL for instance, cost only £1,824 at the time of the V8's launch; but then that was the Ford way . . .

THE ENERGY CRISIS

If any of that was under BL's or MG's control, there was one mid-1970s phenomenon that wasn't: the Energy Crisis. Sparked by the

The V8 only ever appeared in GT guise, as MG reckoned the open-topped shell wasn't stiff enough for the extra power.

Arab–Israeli War of October 1973 (the 'Yom Kippur War'), and the long-term effects that had on already dwindling oil supplies to the West, the Energy Crisis could not have been worse timed for the V8.

In reality, it wasn't a particularly thirsty car at all, most testers were very complimentary and consumption figures in the mid-20s mpg (very little different from the four-cylinder GT) were about par for the course. Long-legged gearing which gave 28.5mph (46kph)/1,000rpm in overdrive top meaning a leisurely 2,460rpm for 70mph (112kph) helped considerably in achieving that.

Actual figures and perceived difficulties are quite different things, of course, and it was very hard for BL or MG to disassociate 'V8' from 'thirsty' in the public mind.

But probably no one thing cut short the V8: the lack of an American market, the price, the ever-less-forgivable longness-in-the-tooth of the basic package, the Energy Crisis, the new competition, were all factors.

In the few remaining months of 1973, Abingdon turned out 1,069 V8s – and that was the most that ever left the works in a calendar year. There were 854 in 1974, 489 in 1975 and just 176 in 1976 – most of those going to University Motors. That meant a total of 2,591 examples of the fastest post-war production car MG ever built; of the car that had all the basic ingredients to turn the decline of the B around.

There was never much time for modifications, save for the common change to 'rubber bumper' spec at the end of 1973, even though the model was never going anywhere near the USA.

Eventually, BL invoked the excuse of insufficient engine supplies – which, in fairness, was partly true, but not, as later events showed insurmountable. It at least gave the V8 an honourable discharge of sorts.

In September 1973, the last MGB GT V8 rolled off the lines and the B shuffled one step closer to history.

9 Competition History

Throughout their history, MG have had a relationship with motor sport that has had very little to do with their own ambitions and everything to do with who happened to be in corporate charge at any given moment.

For a marque that started life with the express intention of making sporty cars, and whose whole commercial history has been based on making cars for enthusiasts; motor sport, in all its forms, might seem like the glaringly obvious way to promote the marque and to develop the machinery. Well, to MG, through men like Kimber, Thornley, Enever, Reg Jackson et al, it was; to their successive lords and masters, though, motor sport was alternately either tolerated or terminated, depending on mood. It would be hard to say that it was ever actively encouraged.

RETURN TO ABINGDON

The B arrived during one of the brief periods of tolerance, when there was even an official BMC Competitions Department based at Abingdon, and controlled since 1961 by Stuart Turner. The Competitions Department had been re-established under Marcus Chambers at Abingdon in 1954 (two years after the formation of BMC), when the design staff and the whole drawing office went back there after their enforced exile to Cowley from 1935.

The re-opening more or less coincided with the go-ahead for the MGA and one of the Abingdon Competitions Department's first projects was the launch of the A, in the guise of the prototype racers which ran at Le Mans in 1955.

It was a debut totally overshadowed by the Levegh disaster in which over eighty spectators died, and when three more people were killed in the A's very next racing outing, in the Tourist Trophy at Dundrod in September 1955. Sir Leonard Lord and BMC pulled the plug yet again on MG's official involvement with racing.

The company kept its hand in, to a degree, with rallying and all manner of back-door involvements (they'd had plenty of practice at covert support) and, of course, they did build the incredible Enever record breaking streamliners which contributed so much to the shape of the B.

And by the time the B itself appeared, the management's attitude was a little more flexible again; this time the choice of events would be dictated more by the adaptability of the B to whatever regulations were appropriate – and that, in effect, meant that the B was destined mainly to be a long distance racer and a durable rally car.

CHOOSING A ROLE

The problem in finding a racing role for the B in 1962/1963 was that the prevailing racing classes didn't allow a great deal to be done with production sports cars, or at least not a great deal that was of any use to MG; on that basis, the B was really too heavy and not powerful enough to be much of a sprinter, but it was robust and reliable enough to be a very promising endurance racer and rally car – and with events like Le Mans and the Monte Carlo Rally to be tackled, there was potentially a great deal of kudos in that.

The Competitions Department also had a head start in preparing the B for competition, in that so much of the running gear, venerable B-Series engine included, was well-proven and thoroughly understood. That might have frustrated Competitions in a minor way, but it suited BMC very well; it kept the costs down and it meant that they could genuinely tell customers that the vast majority of the modifications on the racers were freely available over the counter from the Special Tuning Department.

All they had to do now was show some results.

INTO THE FRAY

For the 1963 season, they prepared three cars: 6 DBL, 7 DBL and 8DBL, all in the 'works' colours or red with white hardtops. They had alloy wings, doors, bonnets and bootlids, and perspex-cowled headlamps. The B-Series engines ran with all the conventional modifications, including reworked cylinder heads, special cams, special manifolds and a single Weber 45DCOE twin-choke carburettor, all driving through a close-ratio gearbox.

Ronnie Bucknum (later to become a Grand Prix driver) started the B's career off in the USA with a couple of SCCA (Sports Car Club of America) GT class wins at Riverside in February, but the works cars' debut wasn't quite so straightforward.

Their first outing was in March, in the Florida sunshine rather than the British winter, at the Sebring 12-Hour race. Appropriately, all of MG's postwar record breaking and a good deal of their racing had been in the USA (where their biggest market lay), and Sebring was almost an MG tradition.

It wasn't a very successful outing, though. Both the cars, driven by Christabel Carlisle/Denise McCluggage and Jack Flaherty/Jim Parkinson, retired with bearing failures. The English winter simply hadn't allowed the team enough testing and they fell victim to oil-surge problems. Again almost traditionally, one of the Sebring cars was sold after the race to defer some of the expenses, and the team came home to prepare for Le Mans.

In the meantime, Alan Hutcheson took a class win at the Easter Goodwood meeting and another at the International Trophy meeting at Silverstone.

Hutcheson was partnered by Paddy Hopkirk at Le Mans, driving 7 DBL with a long, streamlined nose to improve speed on the all-important Mulsanne Straight. In this guise, the B was capable of over 130mph (209kph) and its reliability was rewarded with twelfth place overall and second in the 2-litre GT class – at an average of almost 92mph (148kph). That was in spite of Hutcheson having to spend almost one and a half hours digging the car out of the sand bank after falling off at Mulsanne corner.

The same car, driven by John Sprinzel and Andrew Hedges, was showing its versatility by holding fourth place in the Tour de France rally in September until a big accident halted its progress. A privately entered B salvaged some honour with a fine seventh place overall.

Hutcheson ended the first season on a higher note, with second place in class in the *Autosport* Three-Hour race at Snetterton.

For 1964, there were three new cars, plus the two remaining originals, and the year started brilliantly when the Morley brothers took an outstanding win in the GT class of the Monte Carlo Rally with 7 DBL. Significantly, though, Hopkirk won the event outright in the new Mini-Cooper, effectively signalling the end of the road for big traditional rally cars like the B and the Healey.

That Mini win gave the Competitions

On the frequent occasions when they were restrained from
circuit racing, MG still supported rallying, as here with Gregor
Grant and George Phillips's YA saloon in the 1954 Monte
Carlo Rally . . .

. . . and, of course, record breaking, where cars like EX179, seen here in 1956, had enormous success.

Department an outright winner to concentrate their efforts on, instead of at best a class winner, which could hardly have done much for their overall commitment to the B's rallying programme. The car was also having reliability problems in rallies, with both engines and gearboxes.

For the time being, the conflict didn't show in racing. The B's second outing at Sebring was marginally more successful than the first, with both cars finishing this time – the best in seventeenth place overall and third in class, for Jack Dalton and Ed Leslie.

NOT QUITE A TON!

There was just a singleton entry for Le Mans in 1964, for Hopkirk and Andrew Hedges, and they took another second in class with the long-nosed B – again behind a Porsche, as in 1963. Their average speed was 99.9mph (160kph), and the car was capable of close to 140mph (225kph) on the Mulsanne, which must have said something for the aerodynamics.

Best rallying result of the year was a superb, privately-entered 1–2 in the Austrian Alpine Rally and by this time the car was starting to appear in considerable numbers in the hands of the privateers.

Stuart Turner's plans for a streamlined Le Mans coupe didn't materialise in 1965, but the B had a very good year, nonetheless. It started with the traditional Sebring outing, where a tropical storm left the specialist racers floundering while the skinny-tyred Bs romped round making up time for as long as the floods lasted. Unfortunately, they only lasted long enough for the leading B to

Like the A before it, the B was a natural racer for the clubman,
but it had only a limited racing career from the works.

claim its customary second place in class behind the inevitable Porsche.

On home ground, though, the B scored a fine win in the 1,000-mile Guards Trophy race, split over two days in May at Brands Hatch. As faster cars suffered reliability problems, the John Rhodes/Warwick Banks B scored a convincing outright win, and the other Bs backed that up to claim a 1–2–3 in their class – the third of those co-driven by Syd Enever's talented son Roger.

It was Hopkirk's year elsewhere, proving that he was equally at home in rallies or races, with an outright win in the Austrian Rally, *another* second in class at Le Mans (both with Andrew Hedges) and a fine fourth place overall in the prestigious Bridgehampton 500 in the USA.

Sadly, 1965 was the last year for the works Bs at Le Mans, as new regulations began to signal the end of the era of the true road car. On the other hand, regulations elsewhere swung marginally to the B's advantage, as they limited the modifications that others could make to somewhere nearer the level MG had always been stuck with anyway simply because of basic design.

That gave them another good year in 1966, although it started badly with a forced retirement for the sole B in the Monte. Hopkirk and Hedges ran in the prototype class at Sebring, with an engine bored out to 2,004cc, but retired from the class lead near the end of the race with a thrown conrod. The other B, running as a production GT, finished third in the GT class and won the 2-litre division,

Abingdon, and the Special Tuning Department, had a great deal of experience with the B-Series engine, and the engine for Hopkirk and Hedges' 1965 Le Mans entry shows immaculate preparation, but the potential power was decidedly limited.

driven by Australian Peter Manton, Briton Roger Mac and American Emmett Brown!

MARATHON WINNER

A private car won its class in the Circuit of Ireland rally, and Roger Enever managed third overall in a shorter but more competitive Brands Hatch long-distance race. On the same day, Timo Makinen and John Rhodes were scooping ninth place overall, and both the 2-litre and GT class wins, in the Targa Florio road race in Sicily. Andrew Hedges and John Handley backed that up with a second place in class to give MG a very happy weekend indeed. The ninth-placed Targa car also won its class in the Spa 1,000km, but MG's greatest result of the year came at the Nurburgring in the Marathon de la Route when Andrew Hedges and Julien Vernaeve survived eighty-four hours of racing (whatever the organisers chose to call it) including an early crash, to win outright.

BRX 853B, at Silverstone, shows the standard nose treatment plus streamlined light covers . . .

ENTER THE C – AND THE GT

Up to now, although the B GT had appeared in production in 1965, the works had run only Roadsters – qualifying for GT events by running with the familiar works hardtop. For 1967 they made what looked suspiciously like a token gesture towards running the heavier GT by preparing just one car, which Hopkirk and Hedges drove at Sebring. As it was still to be homologated, they ran in the Prototype class, and finished eleventh overall, with a surprising class win – beating Makinen and Rhodes into second in the more usual 'hardtop GT'. This was Stuart Turner's

last race as competitions manager, as he decided to leave in the spring.

Another type of GT ran in the 1967 Targa Florio – a car that was not quite what is seemed. What it actually was was a light-weight C GT, with a 2,004cc four-cylinder engine, and it ran in this guise in the prototype category, taking third in class with Paddy Hopkirk and Timo Makinen driving. Andrew Hedges didn't do quite so well, crashing while leading the GT class.

When the lightweight GT next appeared, which was not until Sebring in 1968, it really was a C GT – and a very special car it was too.

MG, and moreover BMC, needed it. With the big Healey reaching the end of the line,

Above and overleaf: . . . *while 1964 Le Mans entry for Hopkirk
and Hedges had long nose treatment for the Mulsanne Straight.
With around 125bhp, the car averaged 99.9mph for twenty-four
hours and was the first British car to finish, in 19th place overall.*

the Competitions Department badly needed a substitute that was a step ahead of the Bs. Unfortunately, most of the criticisms of the production C were only too true, so something more drastic was needed. The theory was that although the C was never going to be competitive as a production model, it *could* make the basis of a good prototype, with the tuning and lightening that that category would allow.

So the Competitions Department made a really big effort with the C GT; starting from Abingdon project number EX241, MG and Pressed Steel made six very special lightweight shells, based on the C's new steel floorpan and the main steel stressed structure, but with the majority of the outer skin made in light alloy, and bonded and rivetted in place. The GT shell was chosen in preference to the Roadster for its inherently better stiffness, and that was added to further by a substantial built in roll bar. With big blister wheelarches and the C's bulging bonnet, it certainly looked very much the part, and it was.

Abingdon only built two of the shells up into complete cars, known officially as the MGC GTS. They retained the C's torsion bar front-suspension (but now adjustable from inside the car), and the usual cart-spring rear-suspension but with some additional locating links grafted on. There were Girling discs all round instead of the usual mix of front discs/rear drums, and adjustable telescopic dampers were used all round.

The six-cylinder engine had come in for considerable attention, too. Capacity was increased from the production C's 2,912cc to 2,968cc, and with three twin-choke Weber carbs and an alloy cylinder head this engine was all the things the production C never was – powerful, responsive and full of the sort of character that everyone lamented losing from the big Healeys. It gave over 200bhp at 6,000rpm.

The car made its racing debut with the full C engine at Sebring in 1968, driven by Hopkirk and Hedges, who took it to tenth place overall, third in the prototype category and a sports car class win. The car immediately became known as the 'Sebring C'.

Hopkirk and Hedges reverted to the one and only works B GT for the Targa Florio, and finished second in the sports car category in which the rules obliged it to run.

For the 1968 Marathon de la Route, it was back to the GTS – in fact to two GTSs, as the second car had been completed too by then. The original lightweight car, driven by Hedges, Vernaeve and Tony Fall, was stricken after sixty-seven hours by a major brake problem while lying third overall (the worn out pads actually welding themselves to the discs). After driving for many laps with no brakes whatsover, Fall eventually managed to manhandle the car into sixth place! The second car, shared by Enever, Alec Poole and Clive Baker, was long gone by then, having retired in the early stages with overheating problems.

It was a spectacular but not very rewarding swansong for the works team, as this turned out to be their last official race entry. Once again, there had been a merger behind the scenes – this time the one which brought British Leyland into being – and under Donald Stokes, the racing team once again fell into limbo, although it was not yet officially disbanded. It might as well have been so far as MG were concerned, though, because the emphasis now was on saloon car racing and rallying – where BL knew they had every chance of winning outright . . .

The two lightweight GTSs were sold to the US MG importers and appeared again at Sebring in 1969, but without conspicuous success.

THE CHATHAM LIGHTWEIGHTS

Every cloud has a silver lining for somebody, of course, and in the case of the MG withdrawal from racing it was for Bristol-based MG racer John Chatham. Had the works programme continued, he was due to drive one of the GTSs in future events, and when the programme stopped he turned up at Abingdon in the hope of buying the four unused shells. Not only did he get the shells, but in the end he reckons that the deal he did was so good that he had 'stolen' them.

He built one for himself (registered VHY 5H) as a 'works-spec' car for the 1970 Targa Florio but he had a frustratingly poor race and sold it shortly afterwards. He built the next shell into a road car (registered VHW 330H) which went to Alan Zafer, who was at that time head of the British Leyland Motor Sports press office; now there's a nice little touch of irony for you!

The third car was never registered, but turned into perhaps the most spectacular GTS of all, as a modsports racer for John Chatham himself and with an experimental all-alloy engine that he had also prised out of the works. It was quick but it wasn't very reliable, was retired after a longish first career and then rebuilt again in the early 1980s.

The fourth Chatham car became another road car, EHW 441K, that Mike McCarthy tested for *Classic & Sportscar* magazine in 1983, concluding that it was everything the C wasn't supposed to be: civilised, tractable, smooth and flexible from any revs. The steering was light and precise, the chassis rigid, the gearchange superb. The only thing that stopped it being the perfect road car was a very hard ride. It was what the production C might have been with more development.

Although the works had given up racing, of course, there was still a vast army of privateers racing Bs, Cs, GTs and V8s, both in Europe and in the USA, where Bs have a

Above and right: *The same driver pairing improved to 11th overall in 1965, which was the best result the B ever had at Le Mans and was also the last works entry there as the face of sports car racing was already changing and the B couldn't be made to compete.*

long and brilliant record in SCCA sports car racing, well into the 1980s.

Nowadays, there is endless scope for racing the B and its derivatives, especially in Britain under the auspices of the MG Car Club and the MG Owners Club. Foremost among these championships is the British Automobile Racing Club/MGOC (MG Owners Club) national championship, which is open to any production MG, except the B GT V8 and the more modern saloons. The standard class is almost exactly that, and open to cars which must be completely road legal. Suspension type has to remain unchanged, and the amount of engine modification is strictly limited. Bs are allowed a fair amount of body modification, including glassfibre wings, bonnets and spoilers, while

GTs can use glassfibre tailgates, but the wheel and tyre sizes are strictly limited, which makes for very close and exciting racing in fields which can mix Bs, Cs, As, and pre-war T-types on a typical grid.

The V8 isn't left out, of course, the MGCC's (MG Car Club) B, C, V8 championship caters for them as well as for the rest of the family, with classes for standard cars, modified road cars and full race spec cars.

There's endless scope, too, for all the B derivatives in modified sports car racing, club rallying, sprints, hillclimbs, historic rallies, or just about whatever takes the owner's fancy. Just as it always was, the B is nothing if not versatile . . .

10 Decline and Fall

If reading the foregoing chapters about the comings and goings of the B and its derivatives suggests that MG's problems had anything to do with complacency, nothing could be further from the truth. Throughout the life of the B, in addition to the models that *did* make it into production, there were many, many plans and prototypes that didn't – sometimes because they just didn't work out, sometimes because they weren't strictly needed, often because of finance and politics.

To understand something of those politics, it helps to look back over the recent history of MG, BMC, BMH, BL et al and the way the mergers, takeovers and corporate reshuffles affected attitudes to some of the smaller fry – like MG.

SUBMERGED IN MERGERS

So far as the relevance to MG and the B is concerned, the disparate strands began to come together in 1952, when Austin and the MG parent group the Nuffield Organisation merged, to form the British Motor Corporation. Sir William Morris's (Lord Nuffield's) side had owned Wolseley, Riley, Morris and, of course, MG (plus SU carburettors); arch-rival Sir Herbert Austin's side had nothing much more than coachbuilder Vanden Plas in harness, but under the direction of former Morris man Leonard Lord, Austin had still managed to keep an edge over Nuffield in terms of volume car sales.

Although he never admitted to any special bitterness, Lord, the man who had left Morris on very acrimonious terms in 1936 after an argument about money, must have derived untold pleasure from going into BMC in 1952 as managing director, with Morris (and, of course, MG) very firmly under his thumb. That was the first stage of MG's post-war problems, as Lord made little secret of backing Austin–Healey rather than MG – which, you may remember, was why the Austin–Healey 100 was launched in 1953 and the MGA was put on ice for three years . . .

Meanwhile, the other strand of the story began evolving when the Leyland Group acquired the struggling Standard–Triumph company, in 1961 – and with them came the Triumph sports car line.

From their earliest days, at the turn of the century, Leyland had essentially been a commercial vehicle manufacture (in spite of occasional attempts to find a way into the private car sector) and a very successful one. In the late 1940s a young ex-apprentice by the name of Donald Stokes was making a name for himself at Leyland, as head of the export office, where he restructured company thinking to make a major attack on under-exploited export markets. In 1954, the Leyland boom had reached a £1 million profit year, and in 1955 Stokes joined the board.

It was a mixture of the hugely increased profits and a revitalised ambition to move into car manufacture that led to the Standard–Triumph takeover.

In June 1962, another industry giant, Associated Commercial Vehicles (who had already had their own talks with BMC!), merged with Leyland, and in 1963 the now vastly bigger and stronger organisation became known as the Leyland Motor Corporation. Donald Stokes became managing director of the whole group.

*In 1978, MG could still put a brave face on the B and were
happy to show the latest Roadster with some of its predecessors
and a yard full of cars ready for delivery, but the sales decline
had already begun.*

In 1967, having weathered the British Labour government's credit squeeze, they increased their range of interests with the acquisition of the Rover Company – a move partly undertaken to stop BMC doing the same.

In the meantime, in 1966, BMC and the Jaguar organisation (which also included Daimler, and Coventry–Climax engines) had merged to form British Motor Holdings – and it was clear that some kind of showdown between them and Leyland was inevitable, given the similarity of their ambitions.

The biggest 'merger' of them all, then, came in 1968, when British Motor Holdings and the Leyland Motor Corporation merged to form the British Leyland Motor Corporation, which would eventually be re-formed in 1975 as simply British Leyland Ltd.

That 1968 merger had been under discussion, on and off, since as early as 1954, and particularly into the mid 1960s, when the European motor industry was agglomerating to such an extent that the two British giants in reality had either to merge or slowly kill each other by fighting over the same market.

They merged, of course, but not without a good deal of acrimony. And the new chief executive of the whole operation from 1968 was that one time Leyland apprentice, Donald (later Lord) Stokes.

So, once again, MG had a problem; the 'merger' had been very much one-sided, and the side with all the power was Leyland. Unfortunately for MG, they were also the side to which sports cars meant Triumph, not MG.

Even that wouldn't have been so bad but for the fact that, merger or no merger, the giant new group was actually in a lot of financial and organisational trouble. They desperately *needed* rationalisation, and they needed investment into both new products and new plants. MG's problem was that the new regime, yet again, simply couldn't afford to invest in everyone.

THE RYDER REPORT

From record profits in 1973, BL was hammered by the Energy Crisis, three-day working in Britain and a deep general slump. It was the report of Lord Ryder, head of the National Enterprise Board, which led the government to buy ninety-five per cent of the British Leyland Motor Corporation in 1975, as a means of injecting the finance without which it would certainly have died. The next round of changes for what became British Leyland Ltd, under a new chief executive, Alex Park, had to be extremely radical.

At that point, BL comprised four business groups: Leyland Cars, Leyland Truck and Bus, Leyland Special Products and Leyland International. MG, along with Austin, Morris, Triumph, Jaguar/Daimler, Rover, Land Rover and Range Rover (plus the Sherpa light commercial range) was part of Leyland Cars. The division was the largest of the four groups, accounting for around sixty-five per cent of BL's total activities, and it

'The last off the line'.

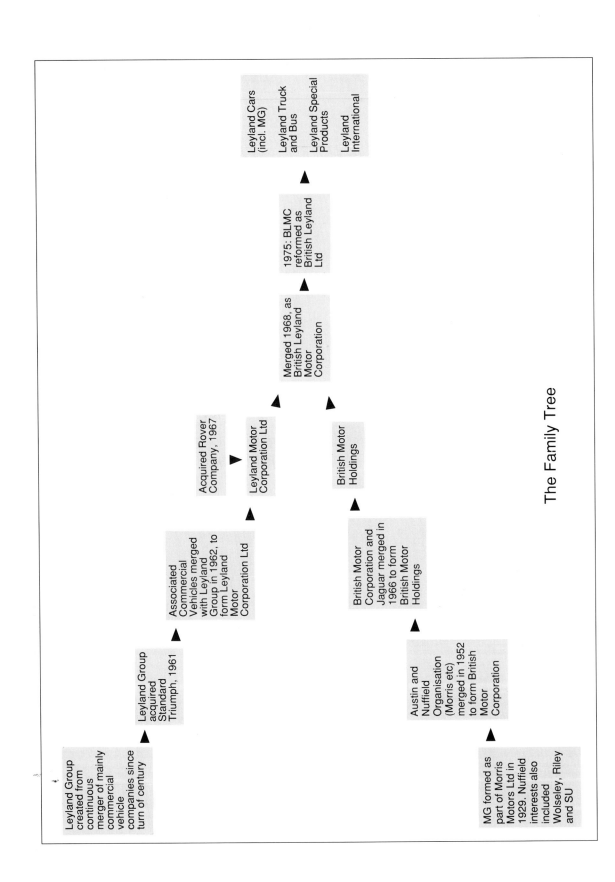

The Family Tree

Leyland Cars (incl. MG)

Leyland Truck and Bus

Leyland Special Products

Leyland International

1975: BLMC reformed as British Leyland Ltd

Merged 1968, as British Leyland Motor Corporation

Acquired Rover Company, 1967

Leyland Motor Corporation Ltd

British Motor Holdings

Associated Commercial Vehicles merged with Leyland Group in 1962, to form Leyland Motor Corporation Ltd

British Motor Corporation and Jaguar merged in 1966 to form British Motor Holdings

Leyland Group acquired Standard Triumph, 1961

Austin and Nuffield Organisation (Morris etc) merged in 1952 to form British Motor Corporation

Leyland Group created from continuous merger of mainly commercial vehicle companies since turn of century

MG formed as part of Morris Motors Ltd in 1929. Nuffield interests also included Wolseley, Riley and SU

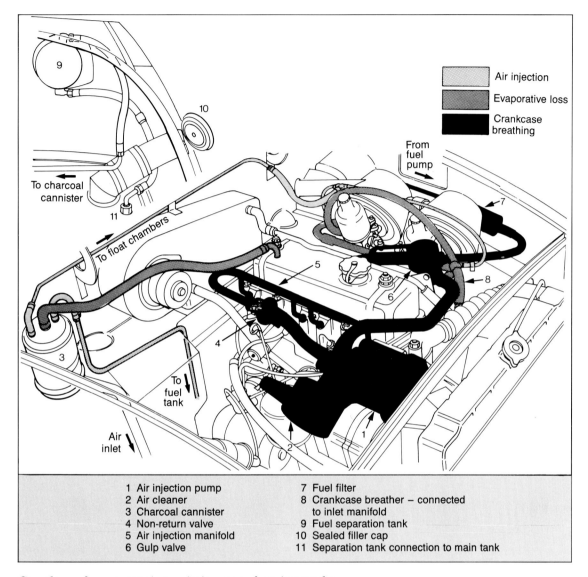

Air injection

Evaporative loss

Crankcase breathing

From fuel pump

To charcoal cannister

To float chambers

To fuel tank

Air inlet

1 Air injection pump	7 Fuel filter
2 Air cleaner	8 Crankcase breather – connected
3 Charcoal cannister	to inlet manifold
4 Non-return valve	9 Fuel separation tank
5 Air injection manifold	10 Sealed filler cap
6 Gulp valve	11 Separation tank connection to main tank

Complex and power-sapping emission control equipment for US-bound 'Federal' cars ruined B's sporting character and spelled the beginning of the end.

was the largest motor manufacturer in the United Kingdom. But MG was just a tiny cog.

It must have felt that way for quite some time. In the beginning, remember, John Thornley, Syd Enever and their team thought that the MGB would have a life of maybe five or six years, and so by the time it was launched in 1962 they were already planning ahead to the next possibility.

THE ALL PURPOSE OPTION

There were early plans to give the B more power and/or independent rear-suspension, but the first major whole-car effort was EX234, which actually started out as a replacement for the Midget. Thornley and Roy Brocklehurst soon realised that it could be adapted as a successor for the B too, mainly

Details of the last production car.

EX234 used wishbone suspension at the front and trailing arms at the rear, with rear-wheel drive.

MG had abandoned the idea of front-drive after the small EX220 (ADO34/35) prototype of 1960. That car, intended as a Midget/Sprite replacement, had definite clues to the forthcoming B in its nose and tail treatment, although it was based on Mini running gear – including the transverse front engine. It went no further because Alec Issigonis, who had invented the layout, apparently didn't like the car (more accurately, he hated it) –

by using the simple expedient of offering two different engine options – small for the Midget, larger for the B replacement. That wasn't purely an engineering decision; even at that stage they knew they had a far better chance of getting the car into production if they could show their corporate masters as much for their money as they possibly could.

EX234 was a serious project; overseen by Roy Brocklehurst, it actually reached the stage of a fully-finished, fully driveable prototype – which still exists and is seen regularly at MG events and gatherings. It was schemed entirely at Abingdon, starting in the mid 1960s with two basic floorpans on an 87in (220cm) wheelbase and with Hydrolastic suspension. That would not only please the corporation, but the chassis engineers, perhaps surprisingly, really quite liked Hydrolastic for its ability to give a decent ride while still having good suspension control.

and in any case, the Mini-Cooper was just around the corner.

SO CLOSE TO PRODUCTION

EX234 didn't go into production either, but one of the two floorpan-chassis was sent to Pininfarina in 1968, where it was given a fully-trimmed body to MG's own designs. It was a pretty little car, a 2 + 2 roadster with even more room inside than the B, in spite of its four-inch shorter wheelbase. The one example that was built was given the smaller, 1,275cc engine which would have equated to the Midget (the B successor would still have used the 1,798cc B-Series at this stage of planning), but the two sides of the body showed the two different trim treatments that would have distinguished large- and small-engined variants.

The level of finish of Pininfarina's EX234 prototype, especially the marvellously neat and complete interior, suggest that this car came very close indeed to being a production model. What probably killed it was not any shortcoming in concept or design, but simply bad timing. In 1968 the company was at full stretch just trying to keep existing models (and particularly the open-topped B) one step

ahead of ever more complicated and hard-to-meet US legislation. Abingdon was also responsible for this facet of engineering for the whole group. In a nutshell, BL couldn't afford to replace the B but they couldn't afford to lose it either; it was still simply doing too well in the USA for that.

And then, of course, with the Leyland merger of 1968, there was the Triumph problem.

Not surprisingly, a review of the sports car options was an early priority in trying to rationalise the new conglomerate's output; if it came to the crunch, the smaller specialist companies were relatively 'soft' targets.

The way Leyland approached the problem was really quite clever; in 1969 they gave both MG and Triumph the chance to submit designs for a 'corporate sports car', to replace

both the MGB and the TR6 – badge-engineered for both marques, of course.

Even though they were apparently aware of the implications of finishing second in this two-horse race, MG went for broke with project ADO21.

It was a transverse mid-engined car, styled at Longbridge under the direction of Harris Mann, but with running gear schemed entirely at Abingdon by Don Hayter – who had just taken over the experimental department. It would have used the four-cylinder 1,750cc E4 E-Series engine and gearbox from the Austin Maxi, or it could have had the Australian E6 engine in either 2.2- or 2.6-litre form, which would have opened up the possibility of several different models of varying performance.

Two suspension layouts were considered; both used a conventional MacPherson strut layout at the front, and both used a De Dion rear, with coil spring/damper units, but one had the De Dion tube ahead of the driveline, the other used it more conventionally, behind the driveline.

This was all largely academic; although the first suspension layout was tried out on the rear of a modified B, ADO21 itself never progressed beyond a full-size styling mock-up, shown in November 1970.

'MR MG' RETIRES

It is probably fair to say that the project wouldn't even have reached this stage except for another MG milestone which occurred in 1969, when John Thornley retired, due to serious ill-health.

Thornley, almost universally known as 'Mr MG', had been with the company for thirty-eight years, the last seventeen of them as general manager and the last thirteen as director. He was also the co-founder and long-time Vice Chairman of the MG Car Club; he lived and breathed MGs, but he hated the idea of a mid-engined layout for a popular sports car, which he always saw as being an essentially practical vehicle with scope for both luggage and occasional passengers, as well as just for fun.

The wedge shape and the radical specification proposals of the mid-engined ADO21 were obviously too much for the Leyland management to take, too, (and in fairness, they probably *were* too extreme for the vital but ultra-conservative US market).

They went instead for the conventional front-engined Triumph proposal, code-named Bullet. The bare bones of that were given a poor imitation of ADO21's wedge profile and early in 1975 the TR7 was launched. In total contrast to the B, it was launched as a coupe only – and far from being received with the almost universal acclaim that greeted the B, it was generally considered to look something of a mess – and it had endless build-quality problems that would never have afflicted an Abingdon-built product . . .

NO CONSOLATION

There was little consolation in that for MG, though; they had taken a chance on their future with ADO21 and had lost. To make way for the new TR7 in the USA, BL withdrew the B GT, even though it was still selling in huge numbers. But where they had expected the TR7 to pick up the mantle, they were sorely disappointed. For one year, 1976, it seemed as though they might have got it right, as the Triumph sold well, but in 1977 TR7 sales were more than halved and the B, even in Roadster only form, regained and held the sales lead.

Unfortunately for MG, though, maintaining sales was one thing, keeping pace with environmental protection legislation was another.

Their main problem now, and it had been a problem in the US market cars for quite some time, was simply making the old B-Series engine clean enough to sell. All US

When MG lost their internal 'design contest' to what became the Triumph TR7 in 1975, there was no longer any chance that the B would be given the attention it needed to survive.

Limited Edition cars, in Roadster and GT guises, were the final fling, cosmetically dressed up but with nowhere left to go without some much more substantial changes.

cars were now strangled by the single Zenith-Stromberg carb instead of twin SUs, and they had reverted to the small-valve cylinder head (making the valve seats more durable for lead-free fuel), plus the strangling mass of emission control plumbing, gulp valves and air injection. California, where the open car should have been in its element, was even worse, with the need for a catalytic exhaust converter on top of all the other requirements.

The factory, diplomatically, had stopped quoting power outputs for US cars by this stage, but *MG Magazine*'s announcement of the 1980 Limited Edition MGB in autumn 1979 quoted maximum power as a miserable 67.3bhp at 4,900rpm on an 8.0:1 compression ratio. Maximum torque had held up slightly better, with 93.5lb ft at 2,500rpm, but with a quoted kerb-weight of 2,416lb, this B's sting amounted to a rather pitiful 62.4bhp per ton. At $8,550 it was a very slow sports car indeed, all dressed up but with nowhere to go.

Almost unbelievably, US MG sales for July 1979 were an all-time record, of 4,068 cars. That was partly accounted for by ample supplies and partly by a sales incentive contest for dealers, combined with a national sweepstake for a 1948 TC. The sweepstake attracted almost 423,000 entries, which says a lot for the interest the MG name could still generate in the USA.

The prize for the most successful dealers was a trip to Abingdon for the works' 50th birthday celebrations, but they couldn't have known what kind of shock was in store for them there . . .

STILL LOOKING FOR AN ANSWER

MG, meanwhile, had far from given up on the legislation problem. They had the chassis side of things pretty well under control, and in 1972 Leyland (who were heavily involved in government-sponsored safety research), had even shown a safety research vehicle based on the B GT.

This was EX250, better known as SSV-1 and it was first shown early in 1972 at a safety symposium in Washington. It had secondary safety features such as air-bag restraint, an automatically operated passive seat-belt system, cushioned bumpers, head restraints, and an anti-crash bar behind the seats, but it also had many primary safety features – the ones that are supposed to stop you being in the accident in the first place.

They included anti-roll suspension, head-up instrument displays, and Dunlop 'total-mobility' tyres (which were eventually to emerge in production as the 'run-flat' Denovo). There was also a sophisticated electronic ABS anti-lock braking system, jointly developed by Lucas/Girling and AP, but that never made it into production. Nor did the appallingly ugly rear-view periscope on SSV-1's roof, but the alloy wheels did appear again, on the B GT V8.

What SSV-1 couldn't do for MG and the B, unfortunately, was give them the 'clean' engine that was the real root of their problems. Without that, there was simply no point in either developing the B further (and quite frankly it was getting rather late for that anyway) or engineering a replacement.

Engine development wasn't at a standstill; BL badly needed a replacement for the B-Series for more reasons than just the MG; they had cars like the Marina (which also sold in the USA until late 1971) and the 1800 to worry about too.

So, there was the E-Series E4 engine for the front-drive Maxi, which started life in 1,300 and 1,500 forms but which later grew to 1,750cc too, simply because it needed more power. And there was a six-cylinder, 2.2-litre E6 version of that engine for the Austin Princess.

There was also a 2-litre B-Series development around 1965, which kept the ubiquitous 88.9mm stroke but moved the bore centres and lost *all* the intermediate water-

With the B gone, the MG sports car was gone, but MG didn't quite go with it. The name reappeared in 1982 on a Metro saloon, and in 1985 MG showed the handsome EX-E styling exercise at the Frankfurt Show, though that was as far as it went.

jacketing to allow the biggest bore-size ever achieved on a B-Series block. The crank stayed the same, thanks to using offset conrods, and in 1972 there was even an experimental version of this engine with an alloy head and overhead cam. The 2-litre could have offered around 106bhp and the overhead-cam 2-litre as much as 115bhp – compared to the B's 96.

Both these units were inevitably considered for transplanting into the B, but in the end BL couldn't bring themselves to invest in new plant essentially to work on a very old engine.

The 1,750 E-Series engine was also tried in the B, including the modified GT which was used as a testbed for ADO21, which was, of course, designed around that engine as one of its options.

HOPE FROM THE O-SERIES

The engine that came closest to saving the B, though, was the new O-Series, which owed quite a lot of its architecture to the 2-litre overhead-cam B-Series! It could hardly do anything else, as BL's dire financial straits dictated that it be based on a modified B-Series crankshaft – meaning that the famous 88.9mm stroke went on into yet another generation.

It was *not* just the 2-litre overhead-cam B-Series, though, and there was to be a 1,700, short-stroke version too.

It was first decided as early as 1972 to use the O-Series in the MGB (primarily to meet US regs) – and that was before the engine even existed!

There then followed a ludicrous sequence

of 'yes-we-will, no-we-won't' decisions, all largely tied up with BL's continuingly precarious financial position, through the period of the Ryder report, effective nationalisation and beyond, into the Michael Edwardes era which eventually brought the end of the B.

As late as 1977, when the B was relying on the 'Federalised' B-Series engine in its desperately underpowered state, it was still intended to fit the O-Series (appropriately detoxed) from 1980.

In the event, it never happened, as the B, and MG itself, became a victim of the corporate problems.

DROPPING THE AXE

The way in which British Leyland finally dropped the axe on MG could hardly be described as subtle. In September 1979, MG knew that things weren't exactly rosy for the company, but at least they were working on the future, with projects like the O-Series B. And while they were doing it they were about to celebrate the past.

1979 marked fifty years for MG at Abingdon, and that's where the celebrations were. They lasted a week, with tours and demonstrations and hot air balloons and much general festivity. The honoured guests were that party of the most active and successful MG dealers from the USA, the winners of the aforementioned sales contest, for which this was part of the reward. They came with their wives and they came as much as anything else to hear what MG and Leyland were going to offer them for the future. The answer must have come as something of a shock.

The climax of the celebrations was a gala dinner and, almost unbelievably, that was held on the same day that BL chairman Sir Michael Edwardes chose to make the announcement that all MG sports car production was to be ended. John Thornley,

who was there, of course, has said the announcement was met 'with very mixed feelings'.

The nub of it was that the B would have to go, and Abingdon with it. It was probably very little consolation that the Triumph factory at Canley would close too.

So 10 September 1979, the day of the public announcement of the end of MG, went down as 'Black Monday'.

It was a shock, but the signs had been there for some time. There had been suggestions that the works might close in 1977, supposedly because the lease was about to expire, but that was highly unlikely as Abingdon was owned freehold – and BL even had an option on the adjoining land.

There was absolutely no denying the problems, of course. With Margaret Thatcher newly into power in Britain, and with the economic buffer of North Sea oil behind it, the pound was very strong against the dollar, which made things uncomfortably difficult for the export market on which the B relied. Worse, though, was the lack of positive thinking from the corporate management.

BL freely admitted that the cost side of the B had long ago been covered, which meant in effect that all the car was costing them was their material and production costs – which suggests they should still have been making a profit in Europe, where the car's selling price was relatively much higher than in America. Yet the cry was still that the B was losing as much as £900 a unit in the US market, and BL further claimed parts shortages (especially of rear axles) and that old problem of engines meeting US specs.

In the November 1979 edition of *Safety Fast* magazine, MG Car Club general secretary Chris Dickens probably got very close to the truth when he pointed out that the O-Series was already being Americanised and that the substantial performance boost it could offer the B might well be very embarrassing for the TR7 . . .

And just to underline what he was driving

John Thornley

John William Yates Thornley, the man affectionately known by enthusiasts the world over as 'Mr MG', was born in June 1909 in Streatham, south London, not very far from where MG founder Cecil Kimber was born eighteen years earlier.

He was educated at Ardingly and London University before going to work for three years as an accountant in the City of London, with Peat, Marwick and Mitchell. During that time, in 1930, he bought his first MG, an M-Type Midget. Also in 1930 he read a letter in *The Light Car*, headed 'Why not an MG Car Club?', and with the writer of the letter and several others he became co-founder of the MG Car Club.

In November 1931 he went to work at Abingdon under Cecil Kimber, as an assistant to service manager John Temple (who later went on to be competitions manager). Not surprisingly, perhaps, he also began to run the Club from Abingdon.

In 1934 he became service manager, and walked straight into the problem of the production J2s that wouldn't approach the 80mph (128kph) top speed of the press road test car. That involved recalling and modifying almost 500 cars, and taught MG a valuable lesson about not promising more than they could deliver.

Thornley was always closely involved with the competitions side of MG and in the late 1930s he managed the famous 'Three Musketeers' and 'Cream Crackers' trials teams.

He continued as service manager until World War II, when he was called up to the Royal Army Ordnance Corps, reaching the rank of Lieutenant Colonel before he was demobbed in 1945. He went back to Abingdon to his old job, and from 1947 to 1949 was general secretary of the Club – then becoming vice-chairman. In 1947 he became sales and service manager, in 1948 assistant general manager, and in November 1952 he succeeded Jack Tatlow as general manager – twenty-one years to the day after he had arrived at Abingdon. He became a director of the compay in 1956, and with Syd Enever he was instrumental in shaping the whole post-war history of the company – particularly the MGA, MGB and their derivatives.

He retired in 1969 due to serious health problems, just at the time of the BL takeover. John continued to live in Abingdon for several years and was often to be seen driving his 'poor man's Aston Martin' – a bespoke blue MGB GT, registered MG1. He died in 1994.

---

at, remember this short sequence of events: in 1975 the B GT was dropped from the US market and in 1975 the TR7 was introduced to the US market; in 1976 the B GT was no longer exported into Europe and in 1976 the TR7 was introduced into Europe; in 1976 the B GT V8 was dropped completely 'for lack of engine supplies' and in 1977 the (admittedly short-lived) TR8 began to evolve, with the same engine. Significantly enough, the TR7 should also have adopted the de-toxed O-Series engine when its supply of Dolomite engines ran out, but that never happened either, and when the TR7 stopped, so did emissions work on the O-Series.

With that decision, any possibility of a reprieve for the B clearly disappeared.

THE RUN DOWN

At that point, the plan (worked out at a crisis meeting of BL senior management shortly before Black Monday) was that the factory would close in July 1980, Sir Michael Edwardes later wrote in his book *Back from the Brink*, remembering his controversial five-year tenure at Leyland: 'The decision to stop MG sports car production created more public fuss and misunderstanding than anything in the whole five years . . .'

And there was, indeed, a remarkable public outcry. John Thornley joined the campaign to save MG by circulating a letter to almost 450 American dealers outlining the implications of the decision to them – bear-

ing in mind that not only the B but also the Midget and the Sprite had been axed. The letters were delivered with the very unofficial help of the US airforce, to be posted in the USA on simple internal postal rates.

The dealers responded in very large numbers directly to BL and they even organised themselves to the extent of guaranteeing a large, firm order for cars into the future – to which BL, with even more crass insensitivity to the position, responded by assuring them that there would be ample supplies of the TR7 for the following year.

Individuals responded too, and the MG clubs jointly organised a mass protest march in London within three weeks of the announcement – terminating at BL's headquarters in Piccadilly where a huge petition of protest was delivered by Cecil Kimber's daughter Jean Kimber-Cook.

The row even had official support in the House of Commons, where Robert Adley, the MP for Christchurch and Lymington called a meeting in a House committee room on 6 November 1979 to protest against the closure. Five other MPs spoke, plus Jean Kimber-Cook, race and rally drivers Paddy Hopkirk, Andrew Hedges and Bill Nicholson – and, of course, John Thornley.

The meeting suggested letters to MPs, a 'fighting fund' was set up and further protests were organised. The matter was raised officially in the House again in the New Year when a motion signed by some seventy members prompted a full debate.

TOO LATE FOR RESCUE

It was all to no avail, and neither were any of the assorted rescue plans, but in one case in particular that was not for want of trying.

Aston Martin Lagonda's chairman Alan Curtis saw in MG an answer to one of his own company's major problems – the need for a volume sports car to sit alongside their exclusive, and expensive product.

By mid-October 1979 he was talking to BL about the possibility of buying the MG operation, name, Abingdon, B and all, to continue production of a revised car. He was not acting alone, but in a consortium that also included David Wickens of British Car Auctions, Peter Cadbury of Westward Television and (later, when he became involved with Aston) Victor Gauntlett. The operation, including buying the company and financing production, had them seeking £30 million of backing.

The talks with BL continued towards the end of 1979 with some apparent progress towards a deal on resuming production of the B at Abingdon, but none whatsoever on use of the MG name, which BL were adamant was not for sale.

Curtis and Aston, of course, were equally adamant that without the name the deal simply didn't work. It must have been particularly frustrating for all concerned that the main reason BL wanted to retain the name was to put it on a badge-engineered version of the TR7!

The talks continued into the New Year, with a breakthrough of sorts when Sir Michael Edwardes apparently agreed in principle to a joint marketing arrangement wherein a new entity, British Sports Cars Ltd, would sell MGs, Astons and Jaguars. That seemed to be ratified in April with an agreement that Curtis's consortium would build their new B at Abingdon and could use the MG name under licence.

Their big problem, unfortunately, was financing the plan. It was not a good time to be asking the financial institutions for money to build a sports car that was conspicuously on its last legs . . .

They didn't intend to leave it entirely unchanged, though. While the negotiations were going on, William Towns prepared some proposals for a revised Roadster with the GT windscreen and doors, neater 5mph bumpers (which even left space for a tiny MG grille) and attractive alloy wheels. It was shown to the press optimistically decked with 'MGB 81' number plates, and it actually was rather nicely done, but the aesthetics were the least of the consortium's worries.

The US emissions problems obviously hadn't gone away and they knew they had to continue with plans for the de-toxed O-Series engine, hoping for a special waiver for the B-Series in the interim.

They even had plans for their own next generation MG, but they still hadn't found the money even to keep the present generation above ground. In the end, hopes of Japanese money were just as forlorn as hopes of British backing and as their own problems continued, BL simply ran out of time to wait. It must be said that BL did make real efforts to come to an agreement during the summer of 1980, but it just didn't come off.

There were other, laudable, attempts to revamp the car and keep it in production, notably by Malalieu Cars and then by Abingdon Classic Cars, who had plans for a special SEC version of the Roadster, to be built in association with the MG Owners' Club. The SEC was built in Abingdon, with a more up-market interior, including a walnut dash, and a neater hood. More fundamentally, the SEC reverted to chrome bumpers and grille and the original ride height, while there was talk of a number of options, including turbocharging and the one option that MG themselves should always have made more of, the V8.

The car was shown at the Earls Court Classic Car Show in 1980 and several were built, but never approaching the numbers that would have justified continued production.

THE BITTER END

And so production at Abingdon, after fifty years of MGs and eighteen years of the B, began to peter out through the late summer of 1980, with the Limited Edition models as already described. The last cars came off the line on 23 October, witnessed with who-knows-what emotions by John Thornley, Don Hayter and Syd Enever.

Thereafter, the plant was quickly run down until virtually everyone had left by the end of October. The machinery, such as it was, and fittings were sold off in March 1981 and the works themselves, on their 42-acre site, were sold in April, the parts that escaped demolition eventually to become part of a business park.

Making the most of a bad job, BL took an interesting line in advertising the last of the Bs. Under the heading 'Why a brand new MGB is already a valuable collector's item', and surrounded by nostalgic images (including a vignette of Cecil Kimber), the copy began: 'Had you been fortunate enough to buy a spanking new 80mph, MG J2 two-seater in 1932, you would have paid around £200 for it. Today a good J2 can fetch £6,000, an increase of almost 3,000%'.

After explaining how much more fun you could have had with your investment in the interim than by just sticking it in the bank, the ad got to the point: 'What if by some mischance, you failed to secure a 1932 MG J2? Remain calm; if you act quickly, you can still buy a new MGB.

'Sadly, when they are sold there will be no more new MGBs. Like the J2, a B is the epitome of the British sports car and always will be.

'Make no mistake about it: some early models are appreciating in value even as you read. Buy one of the last made, either an MGB Tourer or an MGB GT and in a few years you could be driving around in a fortune.'

In October 1981, just a year after the B had been killed off, the TR7 was despatched to join it, ending its mere six-year run (and the Triumph sports car line) without a whimper of protest from anywhere. The next car to bear the MG name, from May 1982, was the diminutive MG Metro saloon. Good as it was to see the name back, it wasn't quite the same as seeing it on a real sports car . . .

11 Owning and Driving

521,111 buyers couldn't all be wrong; the MGB and all its derivatives were fine cars for their purpose and for most of their period: some better than others, of course, but even with sports cars, one man's meat has always been the other man's poison.

And now, over forty years after the B was launched and over two decades after it went out of production, it is far from forgotten. In fact the B is now firmly established as one of the most popular of all classic cars, with a newfound appreciation of the B's simple sports car ethos forming a welcome counterpoint to modern high tech motoring, with prices holding firm against the depreciation that blights modern cars, and with such wide availability of parts and information that no B need ever again be written off as a lost cause.

That is one of the great attractions of the B as a practical classic. It is a car, unlike many of its contemporaries and certainly unlike any of its more exotic cousins, which *can* be used on an everyday basis without fear of the slightest mishap breaking the bank or the smallest malady leaving you stranded.

As it always was, it is still affordable, versatile, practical and fun. It isn't the quickest car in the world (in fact it never was) but it's lively enough to keep pace with the modern world and reliable enough to use for shopping, touring, work or just plain fun.

And even more than when the B Roadster was introduced in 1962, you now have a choice from all the options that followed it into production – the B GT, the C Roadster, the C GT and the B GT V8. You can have chrome bumpers, rubber bumpers, manual or automatic, steel wheels, wire wheels, alloy wheels, hard-top, soft-top, coupe, standard or tuned, old or brand spanking new. You pays your money and you takes your choice . . .

The choice begins, logically, with the B Roadster, the longest running model, in production from the start in October 1962 to the finish in October 1980, with a total of 386,789 cars built. This is the car to go for if you want wind-in-the-hair motoring with reasonable comfort but very few frills, and performance that is entertaining without being in any way spectacular.

For the driver and front passenger, it's a roomy and comfortable car, with adequate, if awkward luggage space in the boot, supplemented by ample room behind the seats – so long as you don't have the hood folded into there. (And so long as you haven't managed to insinuate two tiny children or one transversely-mounted adult in there for a shorter trip).

The hood is generally fairly watertight so long as it is in good condition and properly fitted, but putting it up and taking it down can be quite fiddly – especially in the case of the completely detachable 'build-it-yourself' type. That has the advantage of stowing in the boot so it doesn't make the space behind the seats unusable, but it does take up a fair amount of space.

The driving position has a vast range of adjustment (although you have to take a spanner to alter the seat back rake on all but the later cars) and the control layout is totally straightforward and comfortable,

with just a slight amount of offset between seat and wheel. And the main thing that will give the car an 'old' feel is the size of that wheel and the thinness of its rim.

The dashboard is real sports car – simple and purposeful, with the matching speedo and rev counter dead ahead and clearly marked, and just a fuel gauge and combined oil pressure/water temperature gauge to keep it company. Whether the switches are toggles or rockers depends on the vintage of the car, but they're all perfectly pleasant to work even for a modern motorist. The only slightly illogical control aspect on all but the very late cars (again) is that the overdrive switch is on the dash rather than in the top of the gearknob where it most obviously belongs. Also, it is impossible to heel and toe with the pedal positions of all the cars up to late 1976 models.

All the controls on the four-cylinder B are acceptably light and 'modern' in feel, so long as you don't expect to spin the steering wheel with one finger when you're parking, and being a Roadster, the visibility is normally excellent.

In fact the B always feels quite spacious inside (just as it was intended to, of course) and even with either soft-top or factory hard-top erected it never feels gloomy or claustrophobic.

So long as you're not expecting any great roadburner, the performance is lively enough too. The B-Series' 96bhp might not be much by today's standard, but the long-stroke engine is an excellent low speed slogger and it is pleasantly smooth for an old-fashioned pushrod four. The B has a very distinctive exhaust note too, which you ought, in theory, to find attractive if you're a sports car person.

The clutch needs a good old shove, but the gearchange is light and with quite short throws. The earlier, three-synchro 'box does tend to whine a little bit in first and reverse, and second gear synchro does tend to get tired at a fairly young age – though that is of very little consequence if you double declutch anyway.

The B-Series engine revs happily and willingly up towards 6,000rpm and there's no harm in using the revs – the engine is very strong and long-lived. Even the very early three-bearing crank will give few problems so long as it is well looked after and not overly abused. The lazy torque is such that the engine largely disguises an over-large gap between second and third gear unless you're trying particularly hard on a twisty road – where you can get caught between ratios.

We've mentioned acceleration and maximum speed figures before, but just as a reminder, about 105mph (169kph) and 0–60mph (0–96.5kph) in 12 seconds are pretty well par for the course. The acceleration is tailing off by the time you get to 90mph (145kph) (especially by modern standards, although the B with its reasonable aerodynamics is a lot better than many similarly powered contemporaries in that respect) but the car will cruise reasonably happily at 85–90mph (136–145kph) if you don't mind being blown about a bit.

The brakes are good for a car of the 1960s (even the ones built in the 1980s) but as with most older cars, braking is one area where age tends to show. The same goes for the ride and handling. When the B was launched, virtually every tester remarked on its supple ride – but then you have to remember they were talking about supple in comparison with the near rigid A. Nowadays, bearing in mind we are talking cart springs on the back and a system that originated before World War II on the front, you might reasonably call it lively, or sportingly firm.

The handling is almost completely idiot-proof. The levels of grip are what you might expect from the relatively skinny, tall-walled tyres, but the amount of feel and response are wonderful by almost any standards, with just under three turns of steering between locks. The car is a natural mild understeerer, with a steady and predictable transition to totally controllable oversteer. As has been repeated a million times, the rubber-bumpered cars with their greater ride height do have a good bit more body roll, and consequently more roll oversteer, but that's frustrating rather than dangerous.

Finally, the B isn't going to cost you a fortune to run either; well over 25mpg is common even when driven with the enthusiasm it was designed for, and mechanically it is a very robust car which demands little more than regular servicing and some mild mechanical sympathy to keep it all in one piece, and you still can't ask for much more than that.

The vast majority of the above also goes for the B GT, of course, given that it is so mechanically similar. The big difference in choosing a B GT as opposed to a Roadster is in what exactly you want from your car. The GT is perhaps more practical than the Roadster, in so far as it does have rear seats – albeit pretty rudimentary ones limited as much by headroom as by kneeroom – and considerably more luggage volume. The rear seat backs fold down too, to make even more space, and where the Roadster has a boot already cluttered with loose odds and ends, the GT has a flat, carpeted floor with the spare wheel, jack and tools stowed underneath.

It is totally weatherproof, of course, quieter inside thanks to more sound insulation, and a lot more secure than a soft-top could ever be, but the downside is that the top doesn't come off, so when the sun shines it is a very different kind of car – more of a sporty tourer than the outright sports car that the Roadster certainly is.

As for performance, the GT, as we've seen, is marginally heavier, but also marginally more aerodynamic. That makes it a touch slower off the line, little different in the middle ranges and a smidgen faster on top speed. The same combination means that it is just about as thirsty as the open car on a

similar run. With the optional overdrive, the B becomes quite a long-legged car, pulling 22.3mph (35.8kph) per 1,000rpm in overdrive top, which means that cruising at the British legal limit requires only 3,140rpm.

The handling feel changes a little between Roadster and GT. Although there is rarely any real feeling of flexibility in the Roadster shell, the GT is definitely stiffer – as would be expected from a complete monocoque shell. The springing is slightly stiffer too, to cope with the extra weight, and the front anti-roll bar was always standard. Overall, though, the handling is little changed, with the same mild understeer, controlled body roll and controllable final oversteer, but the anti-roll bar perhaps gives a touch more feel in quick direction changes.

All in all, the GT feels every inch a B, and even now the elegant Pininfarina lines can turn heads, but if prices are anything to go by, open-top motoring still has the edge over grand touring . . .

And that's really it for the four-cylinder cars; the details change, and the fundamentals changed to some extent with the rubber-bumper cars, but they're still Bs even when they're sitting 1.5in (3.8cm) further off the ground . . .

If you really want a B that isn't a B, you have to go for the bigger engined options, starting chronologically, with the much maligned C. Like the B, the C can be had as Roadster or GT, with the same caveats about choice as for the four-cylinder car.

There's little secret, of course, that what in large part killed the C was the adverse press comment around its launch, about its engine and its handling. Sadly, it has to be admitted that a lot of it was only too true.

The 145bhp six-cylinder engine has none of the character or muscle of the earlier Healey unit, and although the C is quicker than the B (to the tune of around 120mph (193kph) and a 0–60mph (0–96.5kph) time of 10 seconds) it doesn't feel anywhere near so sharp and responsive. A lot of that is because

Above: *On the open road with the wind in your hair . . .*

the C is so much heavier, and especially because so much of the extra weight is concentrated in the nose.

Early cars were higher geared, remember, and therefore even less sparklingly accelerative, and the gearing was even high enough to blunt the six's substantial torque to some extent. On the other hand, it did contribute to what everyone agreed was the C's best feature, its high-speed cruising ability, with surprisingly painless fuel consumption.

The rest of the story is depressingly familiar; with the extra front-end weight, the torsion bar suspension and the lower geared steering, the C feels miserably heavy and lifeless around the front. It does tend to follow the heavy mass of the engine straight on into hefty understeer, and stiffer suspension at the back only emphasises the deadness of the front by its own skittishness.

The shell is stiffer than the B's, but that is submerged beneath the general blandness, and it is probably quite significant that the short-lived and little bought automatic gearbox actually suits the nature of the C very well, making the lazy tourer even lazier.

Lazy certainly isn't something you could accuse the B GT V8 of being. This is the B with *real* performance – even by 1980s standards. The whole concept of the V8 is as good as the C was bad. The V8 is lazy but full of burbling, woofling character – and full of power. It is light, too, and sits far enough back in the shell to restore all the B's natural balance; in fact, if anything, the V8 might be just *too* well balanced front to back, losing some of the B's lightness again.

There were several changes from the B in the V8's suspension too. The rear spring rate was quite a lot stiffer and the front very slightly stiffer, while the ride height was up by a full inch. The V8 has more tendency to rear end roll oversteer (and not just power oversteer) and that can actually override the basic understeer to give the car an unbalanced feel. It is also a lot more sensitive to lifting off the power in mid-corner than the B, and again not just because there is more power to kill. That said, it is a very, very long way ahead of the C, and a good deal quicker, too; a full 125mph (200kph) is about right for the V8, and 0–60mph (0–96.5kph) in only 8.5 seconds.

When it was launched, the biggest complaint that most testers could register was that although it had staggering performance and superb overall competence, it was still encumbered by the bits of the B that were now beginning really to show their age. That and the fact that it was too expensive.

As one of the rarest and most desirable B variants, it is still expensive today, but it is also still quite a car.

Its one major snag, of course, is that it never did come in the Roadster shell, so, unfortunately, if you want V8 performance and panache, you can't have the wind in your hair as well not, at least, from a works car. As we said initially, you pays your money and you takes your choice . . .

12 Owning and Maintenance

Not since the days when the B was in full production has it been so easy to own and maintain virtually any example of the breed. Nowadays, although prices for good cars are rising steadily, just as with any other desirable classic, it is still perfectly feasible to use a B (or a C or a V8) as everyday transport, or as an occasional second-car treat, with very little worry.

The fact is, given adequate routine maintenance and a careful eye against the onset of rust, the B really is a very uncomplicated, strong and reliable car.

It dates from the days before sophisticated electronic engine management, so its straightforward, carburetted, pushrod engine has nothing more frightening to work on than a conventional coil and distributor ignition system. There is no ABS trickery in the braking system, just a simple hydraulic layout working discs on the front and drums on the rear. The suspension is simple in concept, simple to work on – especially at the front where that whole crossmember assembly can be unbolted from the car and worked on on the bench if necessary. (Don't try that on the C, though.) There are no central locking circuits, no computers, no digital gizmos of any kind. It is a simple, straightforward, honest sports car.

When parts wear out or break, they are easy to find (virtually without exception), relatively inexpensive to buy, and normally very simple to fit for any competent mechanic. Body parts are virtually as easy to obtain as are mechanical parts, although they often do demand more specialised abilities and equipment for fitting; and it has even been possible since 1988 to buy a complete B Roadster bodyshell, manufactured with the original tooling.

With that and all the other parts – mechanical and cosmetic – that are easily available from specialists, it is literally possible to build a brand new B from bought-in parts; expensive, but possible.

And to help you through the maze there are the clubs, full of knowledgeable, helpful enthusiasts with a common interest and a wealth of contacts.

All you need to be part of the fellowship is a love of MGs, and if you happen to have a car as well, so much the better.

We've already talked about taking your pick, and the practicalities are really quite simple. Bs are still widely available; finding a B is easy, finding the right B is only a little more difficult. The level of the B's market is still such that you will find cars advertised at all levels – from word of mouth, through the local press, general 'market' magazines and, of course, the specialist press.

If you want to know about prices, by all means consult the listings, but don't forget the obvious course of checking the prices of cars that are actually offered for sale; there's no better price guide than that.

Now you have a choice between several levels of car, which you can effectively reduce to: immaculate; usable; or restorable. That's not *quite* as simplistic as it might sound.

Immaculate might be perfect for somebody who wants a car for concours or for showing, but which might be just too good for someone

An immaculate example of a GT.

who only wants entertaining transport at a reasonable price and with a reasonable life expectancy.

Usable will almost certainly be frowned on by anyone who's looking for immaculate; and for anyone who's genuinely looking for usable, the bottom end of usable can turn frighteningly quickly into restorable.

Restorable generally implies cheap but needing work, and turning cheap into usable can frequently cost a great deal more in both time and money than buying usable in the first place; and turning restorable into immaculate, while by no means impossible, demands both money and commitment.

On the other hand, *buying* immaculate off the shelf might be of very little interest to someone whose real interest is the work of restoring, not the restored product itself . . . and so on, through the endless permutations.

LOOKING AND LISTENING

Having chosen a specific model, the general guidelines are very similar across the board. Mechanically, none of the variants has any major shortcomings – even the early three-bearing engine models (which are now, in any event, becoming few and far between) are basically reliable. With reasonable maintenance, the three-bearing engine would happily run to 70,000 miles before requiring major attention; the other engines, five-bearing four-cylinder, the six-cylinder and

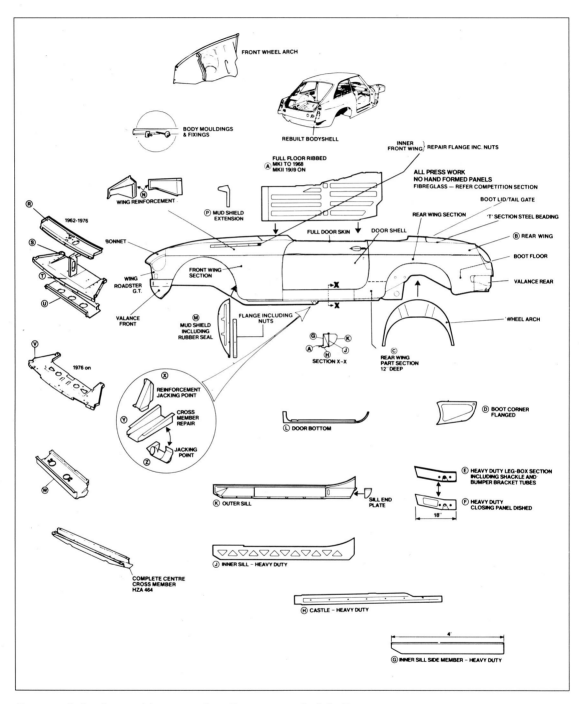

Fortunately for the rust-hit owner, virtually every panel of the B is available for replacement from specialists such as John Hill of Redditch, as here – but the job must be done properly for the sake of safety as well as appearance.

the V8, will all typically last for 100,000 miles before rebuilding – always with the same proviso of their having had adequate maintenance.

All these engines should be very clean and oil-tight; if there is a lot of oil under the bonnet, beware – though the problem is often nothing more than tappet side cover gaskets or the front timing chain cover on the fours and sixes. Oil pressure should be around 50psi under normal running for the in line engines, slightly less for the V8 (but never less than about 35psi), and the tickover oil pressure for the V8 can drop away to around 10psi without any cause for alarm. None of the engines should use excessive amounts of oil, but the V8 is thirstier than the rest (very much so if driven hard), and needs more frequent changes, with filter, typically every 3-4,000 miles.

All the usual basic checks apply, such as water droplets in the oil or a creamy emulsion in the rocker cover suggesting head gasket problems. Listen, too; but don't worry unduly if the four- and six-cylinder engines sound tappety – they run large clearances and can sound quite harsh at low speeds. If the V8 has tappet or cam noise then that is more serious because the hydraulic tappets of this engine are its one weak point and can be expensive to cure. Other noises, like big and small end clatter, should be treated with exactly the same suspicion as on any other engine.

Overleaf: *B prices appreciated rapidly during the late 1980s, but it is today a very accessibe car, from private sellers or specialist dealers, from restoration projects to concours winners.*

Overheating can be a problem on all the engines, from blocked radiators, tired water pumps or sticking thermostats on all, or occasionally from inoperative electric fans on the V8. One other electrical problem peculiar to the V8 is a tendency for the side plug leads to become detached, putting the engine onto less than its full quota of cylinders. Exhaust manifold cracks can be a problem too, but it is always possible to replace the cast components with a tubular system – which can also give slightly more power.

The good news is that the vast majority of spares for all the engines are very freely available and cheap – the V8, remember, is still in production in various forms.

RELIABLE DRIVETRAINS

Gearboxes are also basically reliable, so long as you accept a tendency for the three-synchro boxes to have either weak or non-existent synchro on second, third and even top as well, and to whine somewhat in first and reverse. If this is a problem, remember that it is not a simple nut-and-bolt job to change to the later all-synchro box: the transmission tunnel was modified for this unit's rather larger casing.

The C and the V8 always had the all-synchro box, but with their extra power and torque they do give it a harder time, and especially on the V8 the gearbox can suffer very badly in quite short mileages from insensitive use. It is possible to replace the V8 gearbox with the Rover SD1 five-speed type, but at the expense of originality if that's important to you. The overdrive units (optional on fours and sixes, standard on the V8) are mechanically reliable, and any problems tend to be either electrical or oil related.

The rare automatic gearbox, incidentally, is very understressed on the four-cylinder B and quite a good choice on the C, where it suits the engine's torquey nature, but it isn't

1	Rod assembly	28	Washer-lock
2	Screw	29	Drive plate and ring-gear assembly
3	Washer-tub	30	Ring-gear starter
4	Bearing	31	Washer
5	Rod assembly	32	Screw-drive plate to converter
6	Bolt	33	Washer
7	Nut	34	Screw-drive plate to crankshaft
8	Rod assembly	35	Washer
9	Crankshaft assembly	36	Plate-backing
10	Dowel-flywheel to crankshaft	37	Adaptor-crankshaft
11	Bush	38	Camshaft
12	Plug-crankshaft	39	Plate-camshaft
13	Bearing-main	40	Gear-camshaft
14	Washer-thrust-upper	41	Gear-camshaft
15	Washer-thrust-lower	42	Key
16	Gear-crankshaft	43	Nut
17	Gear-crankshaft	44	Washer-lock
18	Key-gear	45	Chain-timing
19	Washer-packing-gear	46	Chain-timing
20	Thrower-oil-front-crankshaft	47	Tensioner assembly-chain
21	Pulley-crankshaft	48	Slipper head
22	Bolt-pulley	49	Key-Allen-tensioner
23	Washer-lock-bolt	50	Gasket-tensioner
24	Flywheel-assembly	51	Washer-tab
25	Dowel-clutch	52	Kit-chain tensioner
26	Ring-gear starter	53	Tappet
27	Screw	54	Push-rod

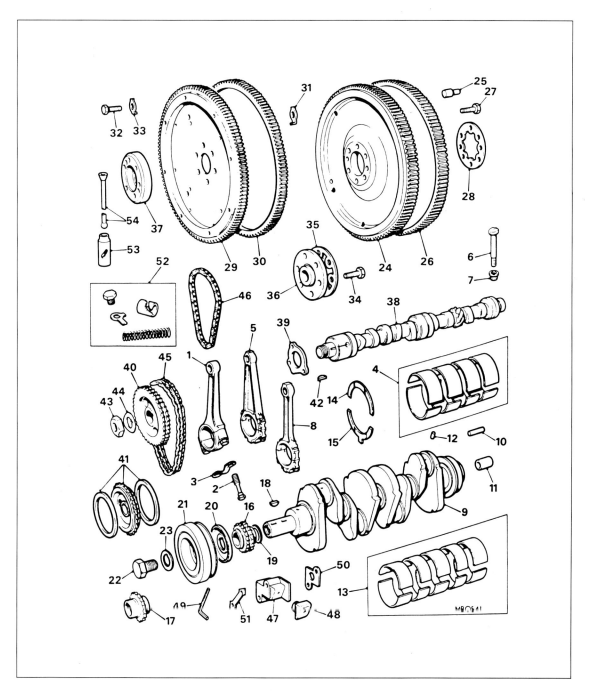

Breakdown of parts for MGB Tourer and GT engine unit.

GTs are generally slightly less desirable than open cars, but have the advantage of the chassis strength being shared by the roof – rust is still something to be avoided.

B GT V8 is now among the most desirable of Bs, but has its own special problems thanks to the additional power. Like most Bs, though, it is perfectly reliable given proper maintenance.

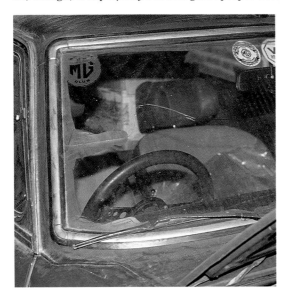

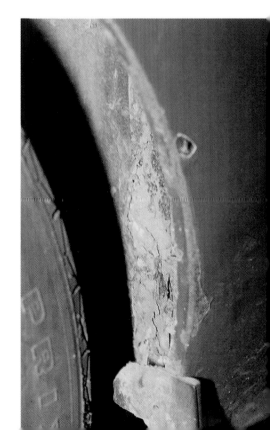

*Obvious rust areas are around the
headlamps, along tops of wings,
bottoms of doors, and in wheelarches.
Sills are the biggest potential problem
as they provide most of the chassis
strength, especially in the Roadster.*

the smoothest or quickest changing of automatics and if anything does go wrong it usually requires even more specialised help than a manual gearbox.

Finally in the driveline, the earlier back axles are the noisiest (that's why they were changed), but mild clonking in any of the axles is only a sign of the relatively large running tolerances, not necessarily of imminent failure. Big noises are a different matter, and bear in mind that, just as with the gearboxes, C and V8 axles do have a much harder life. On the more positive side, unlike with a change of gearbox, changing from early to late rear axles is basically straightforward.

The front suspension on all the Bs and the V8 is virtually identical; on the C it is the totally different torsion bar set-up to make room for the big engine. Yet again, the coil spring type is very reliable but *is* prone to getting tired with high mileages – and when it does so the pleasant feel of the cars tends to disappear, being replaced by a general vagueness of response. Wheel bearings and kingpins are often the source of such problems, but it has to be said that the old-fashioned lever dampers aren't exactly long lived either. The C's telescopics are very much better.

Unfortunately, they are about the only thing about the C that is. It is far more prone to kingpin failure (these units are peculiar to the C) and basically it just needs a lot of regular attention with the grease gun. The C's front disc brakes also have a reputation for squealing which isn't shared by the B or the V8, but all the models are prone to mild disc scoring – if it's any worse than mild it becomes a replacement job. All the rear suspensions are so simple that there's really little to watch out for except normal wear and tear, particularly, again, in the lever dampers.

If you aren't completely committed to originality, of course, it is a relatively easy matter to fit a telescopic damper conversion.

THE BODYSHELL

And now the bad news; well, relatively anyway, although it need never be the end of the line. In a nutshell, Bs do rust, and when they do, being a unit construction car, you can have big problems.

All the models tend to be afflicted in similar areas, but the problem is substantially more serious in the Roadster which, with a large hole where the strength of the roof ought to be, relies entirely on the strength below the waistline.

In the case of the B, that effectively means in the sills and the central tunnel, and in cases where the sills are far enough gone, it is not unknown for a Roadster literally to fold in the middle – especially when being jacked up with the doors open. The GT has the roof strength to make that less critical, of course, but rot in the sills should *never* be ignored, and should certainly never just be covered with new outer sills in the belief that that solves anything.

The problem is mainly one of water and mud getting into the wrong places – notably the box sections of the sills. The rust then eats its way outwards and by the time you see it, the complex (and strength giving) inner sections of the sill will already be far gone. From there, the rust can spread into the bottoms of the front and rear wings, and several other areas are prone to attack from this creeping lightness: the tops of the front wings after mud has collected on the 'shelf' between inner and outer skins; the rear wing tops; the floor around the sills; the battery boxes on twin-six-volt cars; the petrol tanks; the area around the rear spring hangers; the rear valance; the body behind the chrome trim strips; the bottoms of the doors (which also have a tendency to split their skins just below the rear edge of the quarter-light).

The good news, on the other hand, is that virtually every panel on the B is available as a ready made replacement which just needs welding into place (or in the case of many

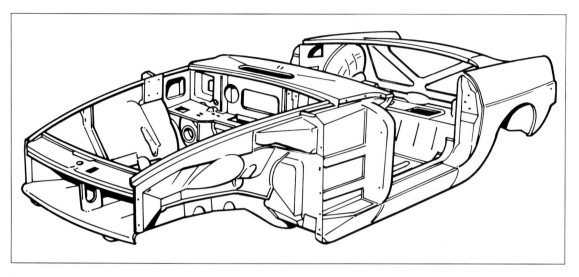

Since early 1988, it has been possible to start from absolute basics with the B Roadster, using a complete new bodyshell from British Motor Heritage, built using original tooling and assembly jigs.

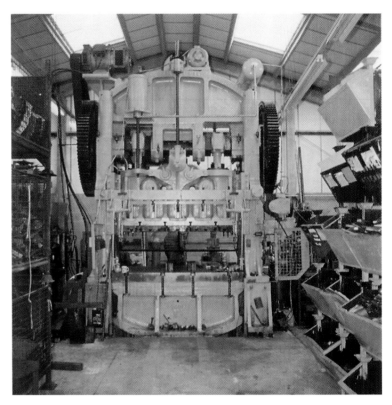

The British Motor
Heritage factory floor.

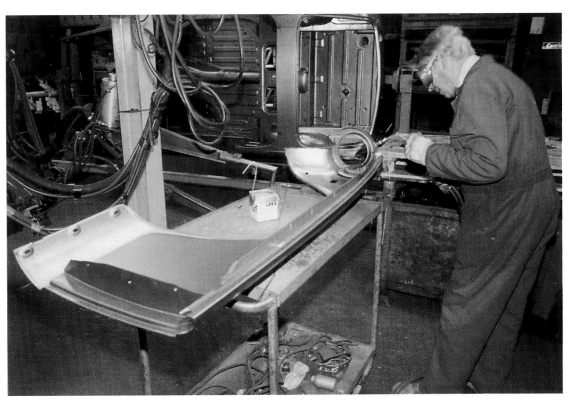

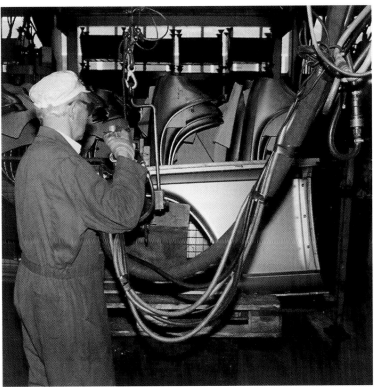

The Clubs

On 5 September 1930, *The Light Car* magazine published a letter from one Roy Marsh, under the heading 'Why not an MG Car Club?' John Thornley, already an MG owner but still an accountant, contacted Marsh to offer his services as club secretary, while the letter was also brought to Cecil Kimber's attention, by journalist Harold Hastings.

The first meeting took place on 12 October 1930, with a founder membership of around thirty owners, and the club was simply called the MG Car Club. It quickly became very active and ambitious, organising competitive events, social events and some challenging tours for MG cars and drivers. Cecil Kimber became a staunch supporter of the club, as did many of the racing drivers associated with the marque, and even Lord Nuffield, as patron of the club, was a regular guest at bigger club functions in the 1930s.

Centres were formed all around Britain and the membership spread worldwide through the 1930s. By 1932 there were over 200 members and by the outbreak of World War II there were almost 2,000 – and, of course, John Thornley was running the club, with total professionalism, from Abingdon.

From early days, the club had its own publication, *The MaGazine*, which changed to *The Sports Car* early in 1935.

The club and its spirit survived the war, and when John Thornley returned to Abingdon, it was ready to flourish again. As sales of MGs took off in the USA, so did the club. From having to carry club news in the Nuffield magazine *Motoring* immediately after the war, the club got its own magazine once again in the late 1950s, with *Safety Fast*, edited by the late Wilson McComb, doyen of MG historians.

Like the company, the club suffered when ownership changed. In 1968, when the BL era began, Thornley was instructed to close the club down, as a money-saving measure. Instead, it went independent and instead of laying down and dying it grew steadily through the 1970s; once again, the parent management had underestimated the fierce loyalty of MG enthusiasts. They were given a clear indication of feelings in September 1979, however, when the announcement was made that Abingdon would soon close. With the much younger MG Owners Club, the MG Car Club did everything possible to change the situation, and if nothing else they at least saved the MG name.

The other MG club that was involved in that campaign, the MG Owners Club, was formed only in 1973, but its growth was even more spectacular than the original club's and nowadays it is the biggest one-make car club in the world, with a membership of well over 50,000. There were times when the two clubs didn't see eye to eye, and they are certainly very different in character – the Car Club much more involved with older MGs and with a much longer tradition, the Owners Club largely for people with 'modern' MGs such as the B, C, V8 and the Midget and with a much more practical slant. Happily, they soon realised there was room in the MG world for both of them, and now they exist with a friendly rivalry.

Where the MG Car Club started with a letter in *The Light Car*, the MG Owners Club started with an ad in *Exchange & Mart*. It was started by former office equipment salesman Roche Bentley with the express philosophy of providing useful services to members – starting with a used parts location scheme. The club has succeeded because it has given people what they want – in exactly the same way as the MG Car Club did, but what people want in the 1980s is different to what they wanted in the 1930s. The Owners Club is a much more commercially oriented organisation. It sells services that members need at prices they couldn't find elsewhere, and everyone benefits. Those services now include specialist insurance, restoration and maintenance services, parts and mail order. And just like its older cousin, it has a thriving social and racing side too. With its headquarters in Swavesey, Cambridgeshire, the Owners Club, too, has centres all over Britain and the rest of the world, and they have their own magazine, *Enjoying MG*.

And that, in the end, is what both clubs and all the hundreds of other MG organisations around the world are really all about.

outer skin panels like the front wings, simply bolting on). And because replacement panels are a very competitive market, prices are generally very, very reasonable.

One point that *must* be emphasised, though, is never try to minimise the repair; if you are cutting out rust, cut out *all* the rust, and that often means going back quite a long way to find totally sound metal. If you don't do this, the new panel will be no stronger than what it is attached to and in a very short time you will be replacing it all again. And the other thing is, if you are not a competent welder, find someone who is: a poor quality weld has no strength at all and is every bit as dangerous as a rusted out panel.

THE ULTIMATE PARTS SWAP

The final option with the B (or the Roadster at least) when all else fails is to replace the entire body shell – or to look at it a different way, build all your existing components *onto* a new body shell. That has now been made possible by British Motor Heritage, who launched their answer to many a B-owner's

prayer in April 1988, and soon afterwards showed how a complete car could be built onto it in no time at all, at the Classic Motor Show in Birmingham. That demonstration went from wreck to road-going car in a matter of days.

In reality, building a new B based on the Heritage shell requires a lot of time and effort – and a good deal of mechanical aptitude, but it is an attractive option. Their very reasonably priced right-hand drive chrome-bumper shell was made possible by the company locating virtually all the original tooling and jigs for the complex shell, and being prepared to make the considerable investment to set up the expensive welding systems necessary to build it. This, in effect, means that the Heritage shells are genuine replacement parts, not mere replicas, and a car built around one can literally be as good as new.

The staggering response to the shells immediately led to plans for left-hand drive, 'rubber-bumper' and GT variants too, and these continue to sell in large numbers, ensuring the presence on our roads of smart MGBs for years to come. It is likely that well into its second half-century the B will still be one of the most popular and well-loved classic cars.

Longwall Street, Oxford.

Still a classic . . .

Why  ?

Out of compliment to SIR WILLIAM MORRIS, Bart., we named our production the M.G. Sports, the letters being the initials of his original business undertaking, "The Morris Garages," from which has sprung that vast group of separate enterprises including

The M.G. Car Company
Oxford

Index

(Italic numerals denote page numbers of illustrations)